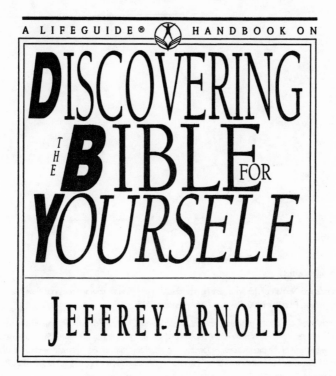

A LIFEGUIDE® HANDBOOK ON

DISCOVERING THE BIBLE FOR YOURSELF

JEFFREY-ARNOLD

INTERVARSITY PRESS
DOWNERS GROVE, ILLINOIS 60515

InterVarsity Press® is the book-publishing division of InterVarsity Christian Fellowship®, a student movement active on campus at hundreds of universities, colleges and schools of nursing in the United States of America, and a member movement of the International Fellowship of Evangelical Students. For information about local and regional activities, write Public Relations Dept., InterVarsity Christian Fellowship, 6400 Schroeder Rd., P.O. Box 7895, Madison, WI 53707-7895.

LifeGuide® is a registered trademark of InterVarsity Christian Fellowship.

All Scripture quotations, unless otherwise indicated, are taken from the HOLY BIBLE, NEW INTERNATIONAL VERSION®. NIV®. Copyright ©1973, 1978, 1984 by International Bible Society. Used by permission of Zondervan Publishing House. All rights reserved.

ISBN 0-8308-1387-X

Printed in the United States of America ∞

Library of Congress Cataloging-in-Publication Data

Arnold, Jeffrey.
    Discovering the Bible for yourself / Jeffrey Arnold.
      p.   cm.
    ISBN 0-8308-1387-X
    1. Bible—Study and teaching.   I. Title.
    BS600.2.A75   1993
    220'.07—dc20   92-34566
                            CIP

16	15	14	13	12	11	10	9	8	7	6	5	4	3	2	1
05	04	03	02	01	00	99	98	97	96	95	94	93			

*To Mom and Dad
who nurtured in me
a love for God
and his Word.*

INTRODUCTION: TEACH ME TO FISH

I'll never forget my twelfth-grade English class at Loudoun County High School in Leesburg, Virginia. That's not because I was a model English student, for I was not. Nor is it because our teacher was unforgettable. Even though I looked up to her, I cannot consciously remember anything she taught in class. My classmates were friends, but I have moved on to make other friends.

Rather, the class was special because a poster that hung behind our teacher's head has been forever etched into my memory. The poster bore this simple proverb: "Give me a fish, I eat for a day. Teach me to fish, I eat for a lifetime."

You have probably heard this saying. But it has taken on a deep meaning for me, perhaps because I saw that poster every day for a year. It made more sense every time I read it. It still makes sense.

My experience in the church has been that we are more than adequate when it comes to "giving fish," but not quite proficient at "teaching how to fish." And this is especially true in regard to Bible study. Although most in the church would claim to be "people of one Book," many are intimidated by the Word of God— even though they do not lack the intelligence to unlock its truths. Sadly, great numbers of Christians don't seem to realize that the Bible was written in common language for everyday people.

I have written *Discovering the Bible for Yourself* for those who possess a burning desire to grow in Christ by directly handling his Word. If you fall into this category, then you will be given tools that, when properly applied, will allow you to draw intelligent conclusions from what you are reading and studying in God's Word. Rightly applied, these principles of study will transform your life forever.

It is not going to be easy learning to read the Bible for yourself. Imagine how awkward you would feel if, having never even held a carpenter's tool, you were told to begin constructing a wall. Tools grow familiar with use, and the principles I explain in this book are no different. Stick with it and use the tools, and before long you'll find yourself reading the Bible with joy and confidence, marveling at the beauty and simplicity of God's Word.

How Do We Use This Book?

This book is designed for use by both individuals and groups. If you are studying with a group, you may want to prepare beforehand by using the questions for individual study at the end of each chapter. These questions are followed by additional questions that could be used to guide a group whose members are learning inductive study together. A group undertaking this challenge will need to meet for ten weeks, at least one hour per week. In addition, the group members should make a commitment to each other: a promise to complete all work found at the end of the chapters.

To facilitate the individual and group study processes, there are three appendices. The first discusses ways to use this book in a small-group setting. The second includes examples of the homework so that individuals and group leaders can check their findings. And the third is a list of resources for inductive Bible study that you can use when you are finished with this book.

You will probably receive the most benefit from *Discovering the Bible for Yourself* if you use it within the context of a praying, worshiping, community-oriented small group of fellow disciples (the subject of *The Big Book on Small Groups*, a small-group leaders' training manual published by InterVarsity Press). You can adapt this course to fit the Bible study portion of your group time. A weekly small-group meeting might look something like this:

☐ Refreshments, gathering, fun time (15 minutes)

☐ Bible study (1 hour, based on the lessons in this book)

☐ Sharing (20 minutes)

☐ Prayer and worship (25 minutes)

What Kinds of Groups Can Use This Book?

A number of different kinds of groups can benefit from the experience of learning to study God's Word together. It can be said that "wherever two or more of you are gathered in (Christ's) name," there exists a group that can learn to study and apply the Bible together.

Here are a few specific kinds of groups that can use *Discovering the Bible for Yourself:*

☐ small groups

☐ Sunday-school classes

☐ training groups for church leaders

☐ new member classes

☐ church committees

☐ groups of friends who want to learn

Remember, all you need are a commitment to read this resource and a willingness to interact with what you are reading as you complete the work at the end of the chapters. You will be stretched and challenged as you learn *how* to study and apply God's Word.

Your Calling

One of the greatest events in the history of the world was the Reformation, and one of its greatest contributions was that the Reformers took the Word of God and placed it in the hands of common people, for whom it was originally intended. This wonderful privilege of handling God's Word also included a serious responsibility.

The apostle Peter speaks of this privilege and responsibility in 1 Peter 2:9: "But you are a chosen people, a royal priesthood, a holy nation, a people belonging to God, that you may declare the praises of him who called you out of darkness into his wonderful light." There are several things we can say about this verse. One, God has given *all Christians* the privilege of being "a chosen people, a royal priesthood, a holy nation, a people belonging to God." Two, God has at the same time shared a vision for what we are *becoming:* "a chosen people, a royal priesthood, a holy nation . . . belonging to God." You and I know that we are still in the process of learning to live according to these realities, but the fact that God calls us these flattering descriptors means that he intends to complete this work in us. Three, a great responsibility is ours, for we must strive to live as, and become, "a chosen people, a royal priesthood, a holy nation, a people belonging to God," so that we may declare his praises.

Unfortunately, the church doesn't always reflect the tenor of these verses. We tend to lapse into the practice of the pre-Reformation days, when priests were removed from ordinary people. We expect a lot from our pastors, and very little from "ordinary" laypeople. We spend millions of dollars equipping our pastors and priests, and not nearly enough empowering the chosen people who are also called priests. Yet in our society where much comes prepackaged for consumption, God's Word still rings in the hearts and minds of serious Christian disciples: "you are a chosen people, a royal priesthood, a holy nation, a people belonging to God." Gradually the church is coming to realize once again that we should be geared toward making disciples who are able to think and act for themselves and their Lord.

And this means that every believer needs to know how to read and understand and use the Bible. Indeed, we can pray for a "Second Reformation" in which the Word of God will again be given to the "nation of priests" for whom it was intended, but this time with a difference: pastors will invest time and energy to equip and empower the people to use God's Word with intelligence and integrity.

That is the goal of this book. If it can make even a small contribution by giving laypeople the tools and confidence that they need to read and apply God's Word, then it will have been a success. May God bless you as you embark on what may be a new adventure—to discover for yourself, in community, what God wants to say to you in his Word.

1

*I*NTRODUCING
THE
*I*NDUCTIVE
*P*ROCESS

Would you like to fly the plane?" my friend Tim asked me, as I nervously clutched my seat in the single-engine plane he had just finished repairing. I didn't answer; I was too caught up in looking longingly out the window as the ground—and my sense of safety—receded.

"Here, you take over. But don't worry, I have control of the plane from my side," he said. Then he let go of his controls. Anxiously I grabbed them, jolting the plane in the process.

As I clumsily guided the plane, Tim explained the purpose of various components of the instrument panel, and I listened soberly. I was scared, to be sure, and as careful as I could be, since I did not know what would happen if I "messed up" so high in the sky. At the same time, however, my friend, a veteran of many flights, was sitting near me, and he was calm. It made me feel better.

When we had landed and my objectivity had returned, I looked back on that bumpy flight as an exciting (I can't say fun) adventure. Never fond of heights, I had taken a risk and had actually flown a plane by myself. I was exhilarated. I had gone to school, and my classroom had been the cramped cockpit of a two-seater airplane. The learning experience had been intense.

Going to Church

Wouldn't it be great if Christians learned the lessons of the Christian pilgrimage with the same breathlessness that I experienced in the plane— if our attention was so drawn by the truths of God that we hung on every word and phrase in God's Word?

You know that the opposite is often true. All too many Christians are just trying to keep their heads above water when it comes to faith issues. And we in the church don't seem able to address the many problems confronting us, especially when it comes to mobilizing the laity to be a mighty force prepared to win their world to Jesus Christ. Many churches are in survival mode.

I once spoke with a pastor about certain problems that existed in his church. There was a spirit of division among the church members, so that this local body did not seem to be a place where Christ was being honored.

In the course of our conversation I encouraged him to deal openly and directly with the situation. As long as turmoil was allowed to persist, the congregation could never become the worshiping, caring body that God intended. When the church members came together on Sunday mornings for worship, they sang joyful celebration songs and heard a word of victory from the pulpit; but deep in their hearts, the people felt defeated. So the church was actually hypocritical—acting joyful when deep, frustrating problems were sapping all real joy.

I suggested to the pastor that he help the people start to work through their concerns and feelings together. Even though the process would be painful, the cancer needed to be removed before the church could once again be healthy.

But the pastor surprised me with a wave of his hand and a comment: "Oh, we don't need to deal with these issues. I just finished a sermon series on 'Caring in the Body' a few months ago. If they don't get the point now, they'll never get it." Momentarily taken back, I let the subject pass. But the result of my conversation with this pastor was that I was led to ask the question "How does learning, and life-change, occur in the church?"

A Complicated Process

A summary of my pastor friend's view of learning would run something like this: Learning involves exchanged information, and it leads to growth. But is this view really adequate for learning and growth?

Try to imagine that, through preaching six sermons, I was going to teach you to fly an airplane. You have never actually entered the cockpit of a plane. But sitting outside our church is a plane, and in six weeks you are to take your first trip.

The first week we talk about the various parts of the plane, and I remember to bring visual aids (by the way, since this is church you are not taking notes). The second week I describe how to start a plane and work the controls. The third week we look at the maps and charts that are necessary for navigation. On the fourth Sunday we talk about the airport and its requirements and signals. The fifth sermon gets into instrument flying in inclement weather. And in the sixth week we look at laws that govern air traffic.

At the end of the sixth week the congregation follows you to the plane and watches you climb in. After awkwardly climbing onto the wing and fumbling with the door handles, you sit in the captain's seat and begin to fiddle with the controls. Since you have already forgotten about ninety percent of what you heard in my "sermons," you can't even figure out how to start the plane.

The point of this little scenario is quite simple: Learning is a complicated process. Think back to the first times you drove a car. By the time you got behind the wheel, you had observed many drivers in action. Even so, your first attempts were probably a little shaky, and you needed coaching. With a cautious teacher sitting beside you in the front seat, ready to grab the wheel should you lose control, you began to drive in a controlled environment that nonetheless was fraught with risks.

The Christian life is no less complicated to master. Learning is an intricate process, and it requires much more than informing or simulating. So if we are to begin growing, we need to understand the learning process.

The Learning Trigger
My own growth journey has taken myriad twists and turns, but if I had to choose one event that awakened the learning process in me, I would point to a friendship. At the end of my freshman year in college I was privileged to travel with a group called the Continental Singers. From the very beginning, one young man on that tour captured my attention. He was very mature for his age, and his inquisitive mind seemed insatiable.

I myself tended to be mentally lazy, although until that time I hadn't realized it. I was probably immature for my age, did not possess much drive to learn and grow, and tended to believe everything that I was told.

At our training camp a well-known Christian leader spent some time with our particular tour group. We were able to ask questions and "sit at the feet" of this person, and I was a little in awe. But my friend wasn't. Often dissatisfied with the answers he was given, he asked deeper and deeper questions, until I began to feel a little uncomfortable. At the same time, I was fascinated. Here was a college freshman asking penetrating questions of a leader of the church, and he was more than holding his own! It made me think of the twelve-year-old Jesus confounding the church experts of his day.

By the end of our summer-long tour, my love and respect for this young man of God had grown deep, and I decided that I wanted to be like him. That has been my challenge every day in the years since. And I have continued to ask the question, How can I grow to become the man that Christ wants me to be?

The learning process has not gotten easier. And it hasn't always been fun. But it has been stimulating, and I am becoming a better student as I mature.

Both Scripture and my experience tell me that you, too, can become an effective learner. God created you to grow to your full stature in Christ. He didn't make you to lie in a crib your whole life. No, you are to crawl, then walk, then run, and then fly! Your personal potential is limited only by laziness, or fear of the learning process.

People Come with Different Needs

Each person comes into the body of Christ with a unique set of life circumstances. The construction worker with four children may have little in common with the retired business executive who has lost his whole family. One person might need to hear about tithing, the other about the victory and peace that are ours in Christ. One needs challenge, the other comfort.

How can all of this be accomplished through one sermon, or even a sermon series? And who decides what is taught in Sunday school or at the midweek services? Except in small groups and the "electives" that are offered in Sunday school, people in church don't normally exercise much choice over what material is presented to them. No church, no matter how big and how many programs it offers, can meet the complete growth needs of one individual.

So perhaps it's time to change our vocabulary a bit; instead of talking about "people learning in church," let's say "church people who are learning." Do you see the difference? The people who learn in the church are dependent on the given structure and the expertise and leadership of others. But the church members (Christian disciples) who are learning can adapt to any environment because their growth is self-initiated. Further, one group comes to _receive something from church_, the other to _become like Christ_.

Christian Disciple, Meet Inductive Bible Study!

So how can you, an individual Christian, become like my friend who got me excited about Christian growth? How can your latent capacity for learning be awakened so that you can become the growing, victorious Christian that you were meant to be?

Proper communication with, and response to, God through his Word is a great place to start. If you want to be a thinking, self-reliant, community-oriented disciple of Christ, then God's Word can lead you.

All you need is to discover how to mine its riches, to comprehend its wisdom. To help you in this quest, the inductive Bible study method has been developed. In inductive study, you take a section of Scripture and examine it in detail. By asking the right kinds of questions, which we shall discuss shortly, you allow the Bible to teach you. The "trick" in inductive study is learning to ask the right questions. Perhaps you've been frustrated in the past because you felt you had to come to God's Word for the answers. There is a slightly different emphasis in inductive study—you come to God's Word with questions, and the answers come of their own accord!

The genius of the inductive method is that it is _interactive_. Rather than simply _receiving_ information, you are gathering, interpreting and applying it. Inductive study is a communicative process, which is why I suggest that you read through this book and complete the end-of-chapter work within a small group of some sort. As an individual, you will be interacting with God, but as a small group you will be interacting with God _while_ interacting with one another in community. Lessons learned through study can thus be tested in the context of relationships in the body.

The rest of this book, which you should think of as a training course, will help you to learn and apply the principles of inductive study. Chapters two and three will address the "big picture," with an outline to help you gain a basic overview of a Bible book before delving deeper. Then, chapters four through ten demonstrate how you can apply the principles of inductive study to individual passages.

The Inductive Process

The inductive process involves three basic elements: observation, interpretation and application. In brief, the first part (observation) involves "taking apart," carefully examining the parts that make up a whole. Interpretation entails "putting together" the different parts so that they make sense as a whole. And application takes what has been learned in the first two parts and makes it relevant to the life of the learner.

Even though this is a book on inductive Bible study, the inductive process is not limited to the Bible. Most learning takes place within the basic framework offered by inductive thinking. My friend in the Continental Singers was a learning, growing person because he asked questions (observation), interacted with potential answers (interpretation) and sought relevance to his life (application). So the inductive process can help you learn in all areas of life, not just Bible study.

Observation

Observation occurs when we want answers to life's questions. In order to receive answers, we learn to ask questions.

Think of how children learn. With their inquisitive minds, quick fingers and utilization of taste, touch, smell, hearing and sight, they demonstrate their desire to build on what they already know. If you were to put their drive into words, you'd say that they are constantly seeking new information so that they can better understand, and live in, the world around them.

Two very interesting things happen as we grow older. First, we often find that the intensity of childhood learning is replaced by stagnation. We rationalize our stagnation with such clichés as "I'm not as smart as I used to be" and "Children memorize much faster than older people." But this means that we miss continual opportunities to discover and rediscover a world full of wonder, challenge and excitement.

The second thing that happens is that because of the busyness of everyday life we stop utilizing the principle of observation. Just take a moment and try to remember the last time you watched a bee in flight (with awe, not fear!). It is very easy to walk by, or on, flowers without experiencing their delicate beauty. And we forget to notice the wonderful uniqueness that God created in each person too. As we get older, we miss much of life simply because we don't observe.

Yet the practice of observation is central to growth. Suppose you are stuck in a job that you dislike intensely. You have two basic choices. Your first choice is to "accept" your lot in life and spend your next years grumbling, griping and blaming others for your unhappiness. Or you could grow through this situation by starting with observation. You may seek answers to the following questions: What is the true cause of my unhappiness? How did I get myself into this position? What is it that will make me happy? What would Christ do in my situation? What do mature Christians do when put in my position? What are my options?

Here is a short definition: Observation involves *asking questions,* in search of answers, so that learning and growth can occur.

Interpretation

The second thing we do in the learning process is interact with the information gleaned through observation. Interaction, or interpretation, allows us to filter truth from untruth, relevance from irrelevance.

To illustrate how interpretation flows from observation, imagine that you have come upon a model airplane partially assembled on a table. As you look it over, it becomes apparent that the plane has not been put together correctly. You are aware that it is a plane, but not quite sure of its purpose (is it a passenger jet? an Air Force plane?).

The first thing you do is use the principle of observation. You take the plane apart and start trying to identify the various parts. With the help of the instructions, you are able to separate each individual piece and identify its purpose.

Then, you interpret by starting to fit the pieces back together. You note interrelationships between small pieces, then larger pieces, and finally the whole. When the plane is reassembled, you are able to tell that it is a B-2 bomber.

In the interpretation step you interact with the information gleaned through observation. If observation is crucial to initiate learning, interpretation is essential to show how things fit together. A man from outer space, upon discovering a helmet, set of shoulder pads, jersey, oblong ball, playing field and goalposts, might be able to describe each part in detail after careful examination (observation). But he would miss the whole point unless he was able to eventually describe the game of football (interpretation).

A definition: Interpretation is interaction with the information discovered through observation, so that the parts start to fit together and make sense as a whole.

Application
And then comes application. Until this step in the learning process, the learner is not necessarily responsible for what he or she has learned. Application is what separates the inductive process from a merely intellectual exercise. We will be held accountable for what we know. When we make application we hold our personal responsibility before God, ourselves and others in high regard.

Suppose that you are lost in the woods, but you have a map. As you wander about you will make observations—carefully examining creeks, trees, hills, valleys and other landmarks. Then you begin to understand the correspondence between the map and what you are seeing (interpretation). After further study you realize that a particular creek will lead you to safety.

What do you do with this knowledge? You act upon it. You follow the creek and take responsibility for saving yourself. Just think how absurd it would be to give up and sit down under a tree _after_ you had figured out how to get out of the woods!

A definition: Application involves taking what has been learned through observation and interpretation and attempting to make a correct correlation with one's life through trial and error.

Moving Ahead

Whether you are involved in a dynamic, lively church or one that is not currently challenging you to grow, you alone must accept responsibility for your growth in Christ. And inductive Bible study provides the tools to help you benefit from daily time with God.

You will discover, in these coming weeks, that meeting with others to apply inductive Bible study can be exciting. There is nothing more stimulating than a community of Christians who are growing strong in their faith. So whether you are involved in individual study or are part of a Sunday-school class, small group, committee or other such group, let's get started!

Personal Study and Reflection

1. Complete the following self-test. Circle the number, from 1 to 5, that best corresponds to who you are or how you feel. The number 1 represents a weak response ("no, that's not me"), and 5 is strong ("yes, that is me"). When you have completed this book, return to this self-test and see how your answers have changed!

When I read the Bible, I feel very sure of myself. 1 2 3 4 5

I understand what I read when I read the Bible. 1 2 3 4 5

I love to dig deeply into the Word of God. 1 2 3 4 5

I know the Old Testament well. 1 2 3 4 5

I know the New Testament well. 1 2 3 4 5

If you ask me specifics about books of the Bible, I could at least tell you a few things about each Bible book. 1 2 3 4 5

I regularly apply God's Word in my life. 1 2 3 4 5

I wish I knew better how to read and apply God's Word. 1 2 3 4 5

2. Write in your own words (preferably from memory) a description of inductive study.

3. What are the three parts to inductive study, and what does each part accomplish?

Digging Deeper in Group Study

1. Discuss: How did everyone feel after the self-test?

2. Discuss: What is one thing that excites you about what you will learn in the weeks ahead?

3. Interactive exercise: Bring several flowers (preferably one for each group member; if none are available, a house plant, tree branch or other object from nature will suffice). Spend some individual time observing characteristics of the flowers, then as a group begin compiling a list. Try to come up with at least thirty characteristics, if possible (example: the stem is thinner at the top than it is at the bottom).

Question: What do your observations teach you about the flowers?

Question: How has this exercise taught you about inductive study?

What did you learn about God's design in the flower you examined?

2

APPROACHING THE **S**TUDY OF A **B**IBLE **B**OOK

I was worried. It was starting to get late, and part of our group had still not come out of the woods. As I paced the narrow road where the trail ended, I began to play out some possible search-and-rescue scenarios, and my anxiety grew.

We had had a glorious day in the White Mountains of New Hampshire. Working our way up a little-used path that seemed to parallel a stream, our youth group had taken a picnic about a mile into the woods. We had sat on rocks in the middle of a cascading mountain stream and enjoyed our meal. Then, as we began to head back, some group members decided that they wanted to follow the stream back to the entrance of the trail. Since we believed that the stream paralleled the path the whole way back, I agreed to return on the trail with those who weren't as adventurous while another leader accompanied the group that wanted to hike along the stream. We had parted ways, and my group had made the return trek in about twenty-five minutes.

Now, several hours later, I considered my options. I could take the car and go for help, but I might be overreacting. What if I left for help and our group emerged from the woods just then? I would look foolish. The only thing I knew to do was go into the woods and look for the group. So I started in, and soon left the trail to find the stream. But having followed a stream for a little way, I soon realized that I had forgotten how to return to the trail. Now I was fighting panic. My fear increased when I came upon what appeared to be a different stream. Which one had the group been following?

Attempting to retrace my steps, I started looking at landmarks. I closely examined each bend in the stream, a particular hill, even trees. I began to find my way again, and after a while I ended up at the trail entrance. Forty-five minutes had passed and there was still no sign of the group, so I re-entered the woods, determined to locate the group and discover the mystery of the stream that went in two different directions. While traveling the stream again I located a member of the lost group who had been sent ahead to find the trail. He had gotten lost and was unsure where his group was, so we continued our search. In the process, we solved the mystery of the two streams, discovering that one part was actually a shortcut through the woods while the other part wound deeper into the woods and then cut back to rejoin the first part.

Eventually, to my great relief, we found the rest of the group and led them to the trail's end. And I noticed something while leading the group out of the woods. I had become familiar with the woods, and I now felt comfortable in its tricky terrain. I knew the stream, as well as certain rocks and hills, and was much more relaxed and at ease than before. If given another opportunity to explore, I would enjoy my time in the woods. What a difference from my initial panic!

Familiar Territory

This story is relevant to our discussion of Bible study because many people fear the Word of God just as I feared the woods. With its many twists and turns, peaks and valleys, the Bible can be difficult to follow, especially for one who is not very familiar with it.

It is easy to get lost when traveling through unknown territory. I discovered as much when hiking with my youth group. Even though I had driven through and hiked the White Mountains on several occasions, and although I knew all the major peaks and valleys, once I entered the woods I was lost. What eventually "saved" me was following the advice that many seasoned hikers offer: find the stream! Water always runs downhill, and it must flow somewhere. When you wander in the woods, it is easy to go in circles. When you follow water, you are bound to come out somewhere.

In the same way, even with an understanding of the Bible story and themes, it is still easy to get "lost" in Bible study. So in the next few chapters we will equip you to "follow the stream"—apply key ideas and questions— so that you can have confidence in where you are going.

Barreling Through

The best approach to use in beginning Bible study is steady and systematic. You will be equipped in the next few weeks with a special approach to reading whole books of the Bible, and it should prove to be exciting and stimulating. But it won't be easy. There is no "trick" to Bible study. Results come from hard work and persistence.

People generally move too quickly through the Bible and then wonder why they get nothing out of it. I became a Christian when I was ten and didn't enter seminary until the age of twenty-five. So there were fifteen years of Christian life in between, years that included Christian service, hundreds of Sunday-school lessons, conferences, seminars and thousands of sermons. But at the age of twenty-five I could tell you very little about the Bible other than stories I had heard and isolated facts I had learned.

In other words, the lessons of the Bible were still removed from my thinking, even though I had read the Bible.

That all changed in seminary, but only because I was then required to work in-depth through such books as Isaiah, Philippians and James (three particular courses I took). Since I spent months working through these books, I can now quote whole passages, and I have learned their lessons well. Seminary in effect slowed me down and made me more systematic, and this "new" approach to the Bible has opened up a world that is very exciting.

Understanding the Units

A systematic approach to Bible study starts with the natural layout of the Bible. First, there are two main groupings of material, called the Old and New Testaments. Then there are what we call the "books" of the Bible, so called not necessarily because of their length but because they are sixty-six separate entities within the overall work.

Our approach in the next two chapters will be to equip you to study the books of the Bible. It is extremely difficult, if not impossible, to study the Bible effectively in the long term without understanding these larger units. Reading a particular passage in a book of the Bible without grasping certain things about the book is like parachuting into the middle of a woods and trying to find your way around.

Think back to your own Bible study of the past few years. What can you remember about particular books of the Bible? If there isn't much, you are in the same position as many Christians. Now envision studying, in-depth, just two books of the Bible this year by applying what you learn in this manual. Your life will never be the same!

The approach that follows is straightforward, and it parallels the method that we will use when zeroing in on particular passages with the inductive method. We will learn to ask "who," "where," "when," "what," "why" and "how." This chapter discusses the first four questions, and in the next we will examine the final two. To help us determine the importance of the questions and see how they apply, we will use the shortest book of the Bible, Philemon. So take the time now to carefully read the book of Philemon.

Philemon

Paul, a prisoner of Christ Jesus, and Timothy our brother,

To Philemon our dear friend and fellow worker, to Apphia our sister, to Archippus our fellow soldier and to the church that meets in your home:

Grace to you and peace from God our Father and the Lord Jesus Christ.

Thanksgiving and Prayer. I always thank my God as I remember you in my prayers, because I hear about your faith in the Lord Jesus and your love for all the saints. I pray that you may be active in sharing your faith, so that you will have a full understanding of every good thing we have in Christ. Your love has given me great joy and encouragement, because you, brother, have refreshed the hearts of the saints.

Paul's Plea for Onesimus. Therefore, although in Christ I could be bold and order you to do what you ought to do, yet I appeal to you on the basis of love. I then, as Paul—an old man and now also a prisoner of Christ Jesus—I appeal to you for my son Onesimus, who became my son while I was in chains. Formerly he was useless to you, but now he has become useful both to you and to me.

I am sending him—who is my very heart—back to you. I would have liked to keep him with me so that he could take your place in helping me while I am in chains for the gospel. But I did not want to do anything without your consent, so that any favor you do will be spontaneous and not forced. Perhaps the reason he was separated from you for a little while was that you might have him back for good—no longer as a slave, but better than a slave, as a dear brother. He is very dear to me but even dearer to you, both as a man and as a brother in the Lord.

So if you consider me a partner, welcome him as you would welcome me. If he has done you any wrong or owes you anything, charge it to me. I, Paul, am writing this with my own hand. I will pay it back—not to mention that you owe me your very self. I do wish, brother, that I may have some benefit from you in the Lord; refresh my heart in Christ. Confident of your obedience, I write to you, knowing that you will do even more than I ask.

And one thing more: Prepare a guest room for me, because I hope to be restored to you in answer to your prayers.

Epaphras, my fellow prisoner in Christ Jesus, sends you greetings. And so do Mark, Aristarchus, Demas and Luke, my fellow workers.

The grace of the Lord Jesus Christ be with your spirit.

Welcome to Philemon!

In reading Philemon, you just took the first major step in Bible study— you got a "bird's-eye view." If you were careful when reading, you probably discovered that Paul was writing to a man named Philemon about a slave named Onesimus, and that Paul was encouraging Philemon to take Onesimus back as a brother in Christ.

If you got that much, then you did very well. But there is much more to get out of the letter to Philemon. In order to truly appreciate Philemon's message to modern-day Christians, we need first to go back and understand its first-century relevance. Determining the "historical context" (placing a text in its original setting) is accomplished through the questions "who," "where," "when" and, to a great extent, "what."

Who

The first question helps you discover who wrote this book of the Bible, who received it and who the characters are.

This applies to any book of the Bible. Although the authors of some books are hard to identify, and the recipients of others are not specifically mentioned, there is at least some clue in most books about authors or recipients.

Why is it so important to understand the author, recipients and characters of a book? Just imagine opening a letter and turning to a section in the middle of the letter that says this: "You don't know how badly I miss being there with you. The miles between us seem so long, yet I feel like I could arrive in an instant . . ." Most people would conclude that this is a love letter, but how would they *know* without an understanding of the author and recipient? In this case, the author could actually be a business partner who has gone to another country to form an affiliate company, or a parent writing to a son or daughter in college. And in each instance, interpretation of the letter hinges on our knowledge of "who."

To be even more specific, it's important to know not only the characters but also their mindset, circumstances and relationship with one another. In Bible study we have to try to move back through time twenty centuries to "climb into the skin" of the characters in each book of the Bible.

Again, there are three different kinds of persons to identify and understand. First, you will want to understand the author, who he is, what he is thinking, how he feels, his relationship to the recipients, and the ideas he wants to present. Then you will attempt to understand who the recipients are, their particular needs and failings and circumstances. Finally, you will want to identify all the characters involved in the text, to discern how they think, feel and act, to learn of them and from them.

For the sake of simplicity, here is a summary of questions to be answered under "who":

☐ Author: mindset, relationship to recipient and characters, circumstances
☐ Recipient(s): relationship to author and characters, circumstances, characteristics, needs
☐ Characters: relationship to author and recipient(s), circumstances, characteristics, needs.

Now let's see how one might answer the question "who." You might take a copy of Philemon and follow as we go through the different parts, or you may prefer to read through Philemon again and seek the answers on your own before working through this section.

Author. In the case of Philemon, the author is Paul. He identifies himself in verse 1 as a prisoner, a person of lowly standing, most likely so that he could identify with the slave Onesimus. He writes to Philemon and a few other people in a church, and he apparently knows them well since he identifies each of them by name. His mindset appears to be upbeat yet firm, humble yet direct. He feels good about Philemon's faith (vv. 4-7) and positive about the sincerity of Onesimus's testimony (vv. 8-16). You get the sense as well that Paul is very close to Onesimus and that Onesimus has gone from being a useless slave to becoming a servant of Christ and of Paul. And finally, Paul writes as a prisoner, most likely because he is at the time a prisoner of Caesar (you can read about this imprisonment at the end of the book of Acts).

Recipient. The recipient, Philemon, is a friend of and, somehow, a fellow worker with Paul (v. 1). Since Paul identifies many of the same people in this letter that he did in Colossians, it's probable that Philemon is a member of the church at Colosse (for more information about the Colossian church, see Colossians and references in Acts).

Philemon is known for being a sincere Christian and a faithful servant to others (vv. 4-7), and he had owned the slave Onesimus. Onesimus was a useless servant in the past (v. 11) and had possibly stolen from Philemon (v. 18). Philemon has most likely heard that Onesimus is now staying with Paul. Since Paul writes in the assurance that Philemon would be obedient (vv. 21-22), we can surmise that Philemon is a genuine man of God.

Characters. As for the main character Onesimus, we've already noted that he was a slave, had met Paul, had given his life to Christ and had become a useful servant of Christ and of Paul. He is no doubt returning to Philemon at Paul's urging, and even though Paul's letter afforded him some protection he must have traveled with fear and trepidation. It was an act of faith and faithfulness to follow through on his return.

The final category under "who" is the people who receive brief mention in the book. Since the church was probably at Colosse, some knowledge of the Colossian church would be helpful (for instance, is there a particular mindset or set of problems in the church that would give us an insight into Philemon?). You can learn more about Colosse and the church there in the book of Acts.

Notice that I've drawn all these conclusions by using an English Bible text, that some inferences made were based on possibilities, and that my conclusions are backed up with specific verses. You can also see that some lessons can already be drawn just from knowing the people involved, even before we've delved deeply into the text. For instance, what can we learn from Paul's dealings with Onesimus? from his dealings with Philemon? from the ways that he spoke about himself and his life circumstances? Just in "scratching the surface" we've uncovered some big issues. Hard work and persistence are already paying off!

When and Where

Once you have established all of the significant people involved in the book under study, you are ready to move on to the "when" and "where" questions. Time and place are important because they help the Bible student to locate each book of the Bible in a historical and geographical context. A letter written to someone residing in Rome in the first century will be quite different from one written to a person living in rural America in the twentieth century. Issues, circumstances, education, politics and a host of other variables are affected by time and place.

You need to determine, if possible, where the author lived and wrote, when the author wrote, where the recipients lived, the times spoken of in the book and the geography of locations that are mentioned. Here is a capsule of what to look for:

☐ Author: where he lived, when he wrote

☐ Recipients: where they lived, what this place and the local people were like

☐ Geography: places mentioned in the book, what these places and their inhabitants were like

In the case of the letter to Philemon, Paul does not mention where he is or the time of his writing, so we are left to speculate. He does speak of being a prisoner, and we know from Acts that he became a prisoner of Caesar in Rome, so we could conclude that Paul was in Rome near the end of his life (although there is speculation that he had two imprisonments, and that in his first imprisonment he was moved about from one place to another with Caesar's household). Whatever his location or the time, he apparently had freedom to interact with people, for he mentions a number of people with whom he had frequent contact. Onesimus in particular is singled out for having had repeated contact with Paul.

You can find out more about the inhabitants of Colosse from Bible dictionaries or study Bibles. Colosse, where Philemon was probably a member of the church, was a trade city located on the Lycus River. A former center of industry, it had been surpassed by other powerful cities and regions in Asia Minor (present-day Turkey). It was primarily a Gentile city and had received the gospel through Epaphras (Col 1), who had planted a church. The book of Colossians reveals that there were a number of problems in the church, among them legalism and an incorrect understanding of the person and work of Jesus Christ.

In order for Onesimus to reach Colosse from Rome—assuming that that was where he had met Paul—he had to travel by both land and sea. It would have been a difficult journey, with much time to think and reconsider options. Onesimus's struggle and his recommitment to his former master, Philemon, become more vivid when one thinks about the fact that he may have been traveling several hundred miles to return.

What

Once time, place and people have been accounted for, it is time to start making note of themes, ideas and problems about which the author writes. Compared to the sometimes extensive work involved in understanding "who," "when" and "where," this part should be rather simple. You need not go any further than the immediate text to determine the author's content. Here is a simple outline of what to look for:

☐ Ideas: themes that are repeated, emphasized, easily discovered

☐ Problems addressed directly or indirectly

In the case of Philemon, the "what" is pretty easy to determine. First, Paul encourages Philemon, through his prayers and words, to grow in his faith (vv. 4-7, 17-21). Then he asks Philemon to accept Onesimus with forgiveness and love.

Then, perhaps in an indirect way, he shows Philemon how to deal with Onesimus—he calls Onesimus his son (v. 10), demonstrates Onesimus's great worth (vv. 12-14), calls Onesimus Philemon's brother in the Lord (v. 16) and makes Onesimus equal with himself (vv. 17-19). Imagine Paul, in the midst of his great concern for many churches, his daily correspondence and interaction with diverse people, his imprisonment, his emotional and physical pressures, taking valuable time to befriend a slave, a person with no rights in that society! How many present-day pastors, church leaders or church members would do the same?

A Simple Process

This has been your introduction to the "who," "when," "where" and "what" questions for approaching a particular book of the Bible. You may be thinking that the process is more difficult than it is, so here are a few hints.

First, get a notebook and label it with the name of the book of the Bible you are studying. You may choose as you work through this book to use the book of Philemon, comparing your answers to those within the chapters. However, I encourage you to work through the book of Malachi, since the homework will be focused on that book and help will be provided in appendix two.

Write "Who" on the top of the first page of the notebook, "When" on the second page, "Where" on the third and "What" on the fourth. Then read through the book completely at least one or two times, and as you do make notes like this:

Who
1:1 Paul, a servant
1:1 Timothy, my son
1:15 Paul calls himself the chief of all sinners

If you keep all four pages handy, you can move through a book rather quickly, noting references and clues for each category (who, where, when, what). Remember that you are just getting an overview of the book, so you don't need to work out complicated texts or struggle with individual passages. Just get as many answers as possible by reading the book through several times.

If you need help on particular questions (such as geography or identifying the author) and if the Bible book itself does not seem to provide much evidence, consult the introduction sections of a study Bible, or open a Bible dictionary or encyclopedia to the name of the book you are studying. You can find specific recommendations on Bibles and resources in appendix three.

Leave space on the bottom of the page to summarize your findings. In the next chapter we will work with these summaries.

It is helpful to think of yourself as a detective, gleaning answers through hard work. If you do the work, you will learn. If you learn, you will grow. And if you grow, you will become excited about being a Christian. There is nothing more stimulating in the Christian life than knowing you are in God's will. This is the basis for joy, that ever-elusive, life-giving force that people long for. So read the Word with diligence, apply it as you will be taught later in this book, and discover the joy that Paul and others write about!

This week you will have the opportunity to apply what you have learned in this chapter by beginning to work with Malachi. As you read through it, you'll seek to answer the "who," "when," "where" and "what" questions. May God bless you as you seek to learn and grow.

Personal Study and Reflection

1. Prepare a notebook for the study of Malachi. On the top of the first page write "Who," on the second "Where and When" and on the third "What." Use the following easy outline.

Who
Author: mindset, relationship to recipients, circumstances
Recipients: relationship to author, circumstances, characteristics, needs
Characters: relationship to author, circumstances, characteristics, needs

Where and When
Author: where he lived, when he wrote
Recipients: where they lived, what these places and their inhabitants were like
Geography: places mentioned in the book, what places and their inhabitants were like

What
Ideas: themes that are repeated, emphasized, easily discovered
Problems that the author addresses, directly or indirectly

2. Read through Malachi at least once (preferably twice), and as you do so write references under the appropriate headings. Include chapter and verse, and a brief notation explaining what you have found. You don't have to include every possible reference, just enough to tell the story of Malachi and to make sure you know what you are doing.

Digging Deeper in Group Study

1. Tell the group about the questions, fears and joys you experienced as you began to do inductive study.

2. Discuss: What are some benefits (at least three or four) you expect to reap as you spend Bible study time learning about the historical context in which the characters lived and learned?

3. Interactive exercise: You can build upon the work individuals completed during the week by

a. "electing" a secretary to take notes for the group's work

b. opening Malachi as a group and sharing what you found under "Who," "Where and When" and "What"

c. summarizing the group findings in one-sentence synopses, perhaps under the following categories:

Who: (1) Author (2) Recipients (3) Characters

Where

When

What (try to single out one most important idea and arrange others subordinately)

3

DISCOVERING THE **P**URPOSE AND **S**TRUCTURE OF A **B**IBLE **B**OOK

I must confess to two things. First, I used to love "dime" Western novels. And second, I cheated when I read them.

I'm not sure when, or how, I grew to love these books, but in my high-school years I could not get my hands on enough of them. I suppose I loved the action, energy and excitement. Maybe I was dissatisfied with the tameness of my life. Whatever my motivation, I remember daydreaming about being a great Western cowboy with a hat, boots, six-shooter and rifle, and even a blade of grass hanging from my lips. In my saddlebags I carried beef jerky, and I lived a simple life riding in the mountains and rescuing poor souls from distress.

Never one to like surprises, I would read the first two pages of each cowboy novel to discover the main characters (I knew, though, that if a woman was not introduced in the first pages, she would come later); then I would read the last few pages to be sure how things ended up.

My scheme didn't take away from my enjoyment. Once I had my overview, I would ride the trails, hunt animals, fight wars and sleep under the stars with my heroes. I savored the stories, and it is no exaggeration to say that I read some of these novels at least twenty times. Once introduced to my heroic gunslinger and reassured that he would win in the end, I was able to relax and enjoy myself.

The Heart of the Matter

Immature as it may have been, my "cheating" approach to Western novels was based on an instinctive understanding that can help us in our attempts to decipher the Bible's message. The principle is this: The sum of a book's parts must equal its whole.

Imagine a typical Western novel: a cowboy, "Pete," overcomes various obstacles in order to marry a beautiful woman and settle down on a sprawlwling ranch near Butte, Montana. The life-threatening gunfights, the nightly mesquite fires and the buffalo hunts are merely parts, albeit very important ones, of this greater story. The various parts of the book are carefully twined into the plot so that the reader is enabled to identify emotionally with Pete's struggles, setbacks, small victories and ultimate triumph. Perhaps he has to fight a group of outlaw ranchers "squatting" on his claim. And then he must deal with a villainous territorial boss and band of thugs who are attempting to gain greater power. And, as is conventional in Western novels, his first dealings with his future wife are confrontational, so that you are left to wonder whether they will ever end up together (unless you read the last page first, of course).

It is important for the author to write a colorful story with carefully chosen images that will leave a lasting impression. Simply stating the skeleton of the plot would take no more than two pages. Stopping with that would be absurd! Humans have a deep-seated desire and ability to paint pictures and re-create settings through the use of words, and a story re-quires this richness if hearers or readers are to identify emotionally with the characters.

So every novel consists of various parts—descriptions, dialogue, sub-plots—that contribute to the overall story. But at the heart is what we might call the "whole" of the book, the one story around which everything else revolves.

In the last chapter we discussed key questions to ask when dissecting the various parts of a Bible book. Now it is important to tie the answers to these questions together into a coherent, cohesive whole, and that is what you will do in this chapter. To focus on this task, you will ask "why" and "how."

The Importance of "Why" and "How"

Imagine coming upon a very large pot filled with an assortment of food items, the totality of which you might describe as "glop." Being curious in nature, you decide to examine this phenomenon in order to determine what it is. You use inductive reasoning.

Reaching your hand into the pot, you pull out a small, circular orange object. With further examination you discover that it is a piece of a carrot, apparently carefully chopped with some kind of serrated knife and then tossed into the mixture. Your curiosity growing, you stick your hand back in. This time you get a slimy substance on your hands before you come upon a strangely shaped, soft, mushy white object. It is a cooked potato, and it has not been cut with the same care as the carrot. Further explo-rations into the glop mixture yield more carrots and potatoes, other vege-tables and a few small chunks of meat.

One difficult part of the mixture to understand is the slimy stuff whose essence is hard to identify but which seems to be a major element in the mix. Where did it come from? Why is it part of the glop? What is its purpose?

Utilizing the sense of taste, you hypothesize that it contains parts of meat and vegetables. You surmise that someone added water to the mix and that the water eventually absorbed the flavors of the other parts of the glop. Getting excited, you develop ideas about the interrelationships among the vegetables, meat and water. You delve deeper in order to figure out what kinds of knives were used to cut the vegetables, why some cuts of the same vegetables were bigger and some smaller, and how some parts of the mixture have greater concentrations of certain vegetables while others are seemingly deficient.

You can become so fascinated with the parts that you forget to ask "why" and "how." *Why* did someone want to cut up vegetables and meat, add water and then mix it all together? Unless you understand the big picture, or purpose, of the mix, this concoction appears a little crazy.

In reality, you know we're talking about soup or stew of some sort, and that explains why the cook put these elements together. And since soup is intended to be functional rather than beautiful, that person put together carefully measured, but carelessly combined, ingredients pleasing to his/her taste.

This absurd example is meant to show how important it is to understand an author's original intent or purpose for writing a book. It is possible to study the parts of a particular passage in great detail but never move out to study its greater context. And this does an injustice to the Scriptures.

Every author in the Bible wrote with some larger idea in mind ("why"), and each one structured his thoughts around the idea in an intentional, if sometimes informal, manner ("how"). Just as it is an exercise in futility to examine soup without knowing that it is soup, so you cannot read a book of the Bible correctly without some understanding of the author's original intent and the way he structured his thoughts.

Why

You cannot find "why" without knowing, as much as possible, the answers to "who," "when," "where" and "what." That is why we discussed these in chapter two. They take logical priority.

Determining "why" involves putting "who," "when," "where" and "what" together so that they make sense. You will need to summarize your findings under each of the four categories you set up in your notebook. Then you can pull them together into a "why" statement that makes sense when put as an umbrella over the whole book.

Here is an outline guide. If you are part of a group working through this book, you will recognize part one since at the close of chapter two you already spent some group time summarizing these findings.

1. Summarize your findings in each category in one clear sentence.

Who:

Where:

When:

What:

2. State, in one clear sentence, the author's intent for the book.

Why:

To illustrate how this works, let's return to Philemon. Before seeing how I summarize my findings, it may be helpful for you to attempt to work up your own one-sentence "why" statement. Then you can follow my logic in the following paragraphs.

Summarizing our findings under "who," we can say that *Paul wrote a letter to a man named Philemon, member of the church of Colosse, on behalf of a slave named Onesimus.*

Next, we can combine "where" and "when" by saying that *Paul wrote from prison to a Christian in Colosse and had the letter delivered by Onesimus, who had to travel far to get home.*

Finally, under "what" the following can be our summary: *Paul was concerned to inform Philemon that Onesimus was now a productive brother in Christ and that he needed loving acceptance rather than condemnation.*

Now, by incorporating elements from each of our summary statements, attempt to come up with your own "why" statement about Philemon. Here's mine:

Paul wrote to Philemon in order to inform him of and prepare him for the return of his slave Onesimus, who under Paul's guidance had become a productive and helpful brother in Christ.

Philemon is a short book, and perhaps you had already discovered the "why" without intending to (although you may have missed Paul's desire to *prepare* Philemon as opposed to merely informing him). But when you are studying a longer book it becomes more obvious why "why" is indispensable. You will find out more as you work with Malachi this week.

One note: You may wonder why the traditional wisdom about Philemon's being about a runaway slave is not in my purpose statement. That is because there is not much evidence in this book about Onesimus's being a runaway—only a few brief clues. We'll spend more time on this issue later.

The Importance of "How"

Arriving at a basic understanding of the author's intent may be a personal milestone for you, and it can certainly lead to rewarding Bible study. But now you must test your author's intent against the whole book you are studying. And that is where "how" enters the picture.

"How" is important partly because it is possible to put together an incorrect statement of the author's intent. Finding "how" requires a disciplined approach that compares your "why" hypothesis with the way the book is organized. To use a simple example, suppose that we had summarized Philemon with this statement of author's intent: *Paul wrote to Philemon in order to tell him how thankful he was to have him as a friend.* If you study the structure of the book with this statement in mind, it should be readily perceived that the summary fits verses 4-7 but neglects the message of the rest of Philemon. In this case, the "why" statement was too simplistic.

Another reason "how" is important is that it will be your guide for *studying the book the way it was written.* Suppose you had developed the following outline for Philemon:

Verses 1-3: Paul greets Philemon

Verses 4-7: Paul is thankful for Philemon's friendship

Verses 8-22: Paul discusses Onesimus with Philemon

Verses 23-25: Paul gives final greetings

Based on such an outline, you can develop a four-part study of Philemon's individual passages.

We must approach this step with a warning. Some people naturally have a difficult time with the logical thought processes necessary to discern a book's structure, so success will vary with ability. Do your best, and if you need help consult the outlines that can be found in study Bibles, Bible dictionaries or the appendix of this book.

How

With that introduction, we can begin to see how the various parts of a Bible book fit into its whole. This is the final "bringing together" of a book before we delve into its parts in Bible study.

The "how" can be accomplished by following these steps:

1. With your "why" statement in hand, read the book completely through, making sure that your analysis of author's intent is broad enough, but also specific enough, to encompass the whole book.

2. Make any needed revisions in your "why" statement so as to make it complete and accurate.

3. With the "why" statement as a guide, write a simple outline of the Bible book, checking to make sure that all sections support the author's intent as you have summarized it. (Hint: Bible editors separated the Bible into chapters and paragraphs for a purpose. Although you do not necessarily have to follow their lead, these scholars have divided the various sections of the Bible in what they feel is a logical way.)

Now we will look at how to answer the "how" question with Philemon.

First, remember our statement of author's intent: *Paul wrote to Philemon in order to inform and prepare him for the return of his slave Onesimus, who under Paul's guidance had become a productive and helpful brother in Christ.*

With this statement in hand we start working on our outline. The notes might look like this:

1. Introduction: Paul, a person of lowly standing, writes a greeting to Philemon and friends.

2. (vv. 4-7) Paul is thankful for Philemon's faith and love.

3. (vv. 8-21) Paul makes an appeal for Onesimus.

   Paul makes it clear that he is writing on behalf of Onesimus (vv. 8-11).

   He emphasizes that Onesimus has been a great help (vv. 12-16).

   He offers his help and strongly encourages Philemon to take Onesimus back (vv. 17-21).

4. (vv. 22-25) Paul says goodby, expressing his hope to visit Philemon sometime in the future.

You can see from the notes that even though verses 8-21 are one complete thought they can also be broken down even more. As you work through your outline, you'll find it helps to break ideas down as completely as possible.

Based on that rough outline, and incorporating some of the "why" statement, here is a brief outline that can guide our study of Philemon.

Author's intent: Paul wrote to Philemon in order to inform and prepare him for the return of his slave Onesimus, who under Paul's guidance had become a productive and helpful brother in Christ.

Outline of Philemon:

Introduction: In his greeting, Paul expresses humility so that Philemon and friends will be humble as well (vv. 1-3)

I. Paul gives thanks and prays for Philemon's faith (vv. 4-7)

II. Paul encourages Philemon to accept Onesimus as a brother in Christ (vv. 8-21)

A. He expresses the depth of his own feeling for Onesimus (vv. 8-11)

B. He demonstrates that Onesimus has matured by coming to faith (vv. 12-16)

C. He encourages Philemon to show maturity as well (vv. 17-21)

III. Paul ends the letter with goodbys and the hope that he will come soon (22-25)

A Word of Encouragement

Making an outline and finding the one main purpose in a book of the Bible can be time-consuming and difficult. Some will struggle more than others. Some will become frustrated as they try to narrow down a list of three possibilities to one clear sentence.

Remember that practice makes perfect. The ideas presented in this book are not "digested" for you. The first time you work at Bible study, it will most likely be hard. But the premise is that you want to take responsibility for your growth in Christ and you are willing to invest yourself in God's Word with the same fervor that some work on their career, golf game or speaking ability. There are few "naturals" in life; most skills come with work. So don't expect to be perfect, or to write your findings with the eloquence of C. S. Lewis or Plato. Be content with small steps, for it is these that bring consistent growth and lead to big victories.

Moving Ahead

This chapter completes our consideration of the "big picture." We have focused on the larger units of Scripture that must be understood before individual passages can be applied. You will again work in Malachi this week, developing your own "why" statement and basic outline of Malachi's thought flow. There is help in the appendix, but use it only after attempting to work out your own ideas.

You may be wondering whether you will have to go to such great lengths to study each and every book of the Bible. You will be happy to know that even though there is nothing wrong with a detailed and careful approach such as we are taking here, you can simplify the process in future study to make it easier. Instead of reading and rereading a book of the Bible before studying its individual passages, you can gain as much benefit from a quick reading and application of appropriate resources.

The point is to learn what it is you must get out of a book of the Bible before going deeper into its passages. Read Malachi, "pay the price" now, and you will receive the benefits for life.

Personal Study and Reflection

1. Continuing in your notebook, prepare to summarize your findings under "Who," "Where," "When" and "What" by placing these four categories down the left side of a new page.

2. Read over your findings from last week and attempt to develop a one-sentence synopsis for each category ("Who," "Where," "When" and "What").

3. Come up with a one-sentence statement of author's intent. *Optional:* Develop an outline of Malachi to support your hypothesis of author's intent.

Digging Deeper in Group Study

1. Discuss: How has your work in these three chapters enlarged your understanding of Bible study?

2. Explore: Either bring an array of various types of books (novels, how-to books, travelogues, etc.) or find some in the place where you are meeting. Give each individual, or pair, a different book, then allow three minutes for thumbing through the books and discovering what each individual's book is about. Let each person report.

3. Interactive exercise: Using group process and the members' findings from the preceding week, decide on a statement of author's intent that adequately expresses the purpose of Malachi. Then develop an outline of the book of Malachi together.

4

*L*EARNING
TO
*O*BSERVE

I had prepared well for an upcoming lesson on "Praising God," yet somehow sensed that I wasn't quite ready. The lesson had plenty of content, and I certainly felt intensely the importance of praise. And I believed that I had an important challenge to present to the class.

Still, I knew that something was missing. In the hour before the lesson I strolled pensively about the church grounds, enjoying the crisp air and birdsong of a beautiful autumn morning. As I walked, I expressed my concern and heart's desire to God. And God heard.

My attention was drawn to a small cluster of frail flowers. Actually, they were merely weeds which on another day I would have pulled up and thrown away. But on that day I couldn't help but see in them a beauty that was from God. I pulled one and continued my walk, and as I walked I examined the delicate blossom in greater detail. I found myself wanting to understand its design; I traced one light blue vein until it disappeared into the stem, and I wondered why the petal changed from a lighter to darker hue at different places but with exact consistency. As time passed and the details became even more intricate and wonderful, I found delight welling up inside of me. And then I had my lesson.

Running back to the spot where I had picked the first flower, I carefully picked a handful of God's beauties and took them with me to class. We started the class by reading a psalm of praise; though it was powerful, it did not seem to deeply touch the class. And then I passed out the weed-flowers. I asked everyone to examine the flower, making careful note of observable details in preparation for a discussion about flowers.

I got some curious stares, but the students complied with my request. Sitting silently, and perhaps feeling a little foolish, they began turning the flowers from side to side and examining them closely. After a few minutes, I moved to a blackboard and began writing as people volunteered their observations:

The top of the petal has a softer purple color, while the bottom is a richer purple.

Behind the petals are an equal number of small green petals that look like leaves.

There are two buds that come out of the bottom of the stem.

The backs of the petals have bulging veins running through them, while in the front the veins are hardly noticeable.

There are six colors in these flowers, with many variations.

As we noticed more and more detail, people began to marvel. They said things like, "If God put so much effort and careful design into a common weed, how much more a tree, a bird, or a human!" We had our reason to praise—God had revealed some of his power and creativity through a delicate flower. Taking the time to examine the flower in God's presence gave us insight into his character and personality.

Smell the Roses

You have probably heard the phrase "Stop and smell the roses." The idea is that when we bustle helter-skelter through life it's easy to lose perspective. To stop, listen and observe is a simple step, yet it requires great discipline.

Simply observing brings us to reality—that there is a God who is in control, that there is more to life than our seemingly insurmountable personal problems, that there is beauty and order in a world that appears full of disorder.

I've already spoken of how important it is to get the big picture so as not to get lost in the "woods" of Bible study. We've learned to note the "streams" (patterns) that are obvious, and to identify landmarks that make the "map" easier to read. Up to this point in the study we have examined complete books of the Bible.

Now we are ready to take our walk through the woods, enjoying the beauty, secure in the knowledge that we will not get lost. This is where the most enjoyable part of Bible study comes. Instead of traveling rapidly through biblical texts we will slow down, observe what is there and react to what we are finding. And this will allow us to discover order in seemingly difficult texts, to find and savor the beauty of word order and logic, and to identify with God's plan revealed in Scripture. In essence, we are going to apply our senses to see, hear, smell, taste and touch the message contained in the Word of God.

Maybe you remember being instructed about crossing busy, or even not so busy, streets when you were a young child. With the feelings of invincibility that come with childhood, it was easy to take off across streets on foot or on your bicycle without looking. Adults must take great pains to teach children how dangerous traffic can be and how to avoid that danger.

My aunt was a cautious woman, and she taught me so thoroughly that her words "Stop, look and listen!" still ring in my ear whenever I prepare to traverse a road. She made me stop, look left, then right, then left again.

Next, I was to pause and listen in case my eyes deceived me. And then I was to cross the road while continuing to watch and listen.

So I learned to use the ancient art of observation. Even though my aunt's technique may be considered overly cautious, it has kept me safe for many years and thousands of street crossings. And this same approach works in Bible study. When reading a Bible text you need to learn how to *stop, look and listen.*

Stop

Perhaps the greatest discipline required in observation is to stop. In our technological era with its "bits and bites" mentality, we have learned to let our minds travel at great speeds, generalizing in everything while special-izing in only one thing (our life's calling). We see hundreds of thousands of commercials, television shows, movies, billboards, signs, magazines and other thought-occupying items. And we become experts at sifting through mounds of "garbage"—irrelevant material—in order to glean the scattered tidbits of information that are useful. We are learning to survive in the information age by numbing ourselves to details and facts.

There is a grave danger in this approach: we can become adept at accepting whatever "jumps out at us" without using our filters of personal relevance and truth. We are becoming more and more impulsive, less crit-ical in the positive sense. So we allow ourselves to be led by creative ad geniuses, slick salespeople and even high-flying pastors, and we put little of our own thought into where we are going. We let others do our thinking for us, even though they may intend to use us for their personal gain.

Why not stop, turn off the radio and television, and carefully examine God's Word in detail? Specifically, to stop means the following:

1. Don't let the "bits and bites" mentality carry over into your study of God's Word. The Bible is not a potpourri of ideas from which to choose as you fly recklessly through its pages. Take upon yourself the discipline of moving slowly through Scripture, which because it is God's Word must

be studied with integrity and great care.

2. Study larger units (such as whole books) of the Bible to get overviews, but then carefully follow up with detailed study of individual units: sections, chapters, paragraphs and verses.

3. Before attempting to observe, isolate one unit of study (section, chapter, paragraph or verse). To attempt inductive study with an unclear idea of the boundaries of a "pericope" (a well-defined unit of study) makes it impossible to draw conclusions that are accurate. The various books of the Bible have been divided into a chapter format with sections, paragraphs and verses. You can choose any of these units as a pericope.

To illustrate how this works, let's return to Philemon. We have already gotten a basic overview of this book. Now, working from the outline developed in chapter three, we can proceed with a careful study of the various units. For our purposes, assume that we've started working our way through a detailed study of Philemon and have come to verses 12-16, which we entitled (in our outline) "He (Paul) demonstrates that Onesimus has matured by coming to faith":

> I am sending him—who is my very heart—back to you. I would have liked to keep him with me so that he could take your place in helping me while I am in chains for the gospel. But I did not want to do anything without your consent, so that any favor you do will be spontaneous and not forced. Perhaps the reason he was separated from you for a little while was that you might have him back for good—no longer as a slave, but better than a slave, as a dear brother. He is very dear to me but even dearer to you, both as a man and as a brother in the Lord.

Having chosen our pericope for study, we have fulfilled the required first step in observation, "Stop!" Now it is time to start looking at what the passage says.

Look

The purpose of this step is simply *to see what is there*. It may sound trite, but once you start observing carefully you will realize how much of the Bible, and of life for that matter, you usually miss. Compiling facts from the text can be an exciting aspect of devotional study.

There are a few things to keep in mind when compiling facts. First, don't attempt to interpret or make application based on what you are finding. Just make note of the obvious. Second, you will need to record your observations in writing, since you'll eventually be ready to make sense of the scattered facts you have found. Third, try to use the actual words of the text whenever possible. This helps you to refrain from interpreting or applying what you see. Fourth—and this requires great discipline—observe *only what is in the passage in front of you*, even if you are tempted to begin applying your knowledge from other parts of Scripture. And fifth, don't fret when you struggle and make mistakes.

To illustrate the fact-finding that you will do, we return to Philemon 12-16, recorded above. Read these verses and attempt to record at least seven of your own observations below. A few observations are already recorded in order to help you get started.

Philemon 12-16: Observations

  1. Somebody is being sent (v. 12)
  2. Somebody is the sender (v. 12)
  3. The one being sent is "my very heart" of the sender (v. 12)
  4.
  5.
  6.
  7.
  8.
  9.
  10.

Some of the facts you find may seem mundane and obvious, but as you go deeper you will start to uncover those that are profound and life-changing. There are a great many observations to be made from this passage, but here is a partial sampling to which you can compare your own findings.

Philemon 12-16: Observations

V. 12: Somebody is being sent; somebody is the sender; the one being sent is "my very heart" to the sender; somebody is to receive the one being sent; "you" is the one to whom this message is addressed; the one being sent is "coming back" to the receiver, meaning that they had a prior relationship.

V. 13: The author wanted to keep the one being sent; the author wanted to keep the one being sent because he was helping him; the author was in chains; the author was in chains for the gospel; the one being sent would have taken the place of the recipient at the side of the author; the one being sent is a "he"; the author needed help.

V. 14: The author did not want to act without the recipient's consent; the author wanted the recipient's favor to be spontaneous and not forced; the author was sensitive to the recipient's motivations and responses.

V. 15: The author speculated that the one being sent was separated from the recipient so that he could have the one being sent back "for good"; the recipient and one being sent had been separated for a little while.

V. 16: The one being sent was the recipient's slave; the author speculates (from previous verse) that the one being sent will no longer be the recipient's slave, but a brother; a brother is better than a slave; the one being sent will be more than a brother, a "dear brother"; the one being sent is very dear to the author; the one being sent will be even dearer to the recipient; the one being sent is a man; the one being sent will be a "dearer man" compared with his previous history; the one being sent is a brother in the Lord to the recipient.

Notice a few things from the above observations. First, they don't presume knowledge of the characters, even though it is easy to discover answers from the surrounding context. Second, they use the exact words of the text as often as possible. And third, they offer no conclusions unless conclusions are given by the text.

One final item of importance about uncovering the facts: the biggest mistake people make is trying to jump too quickly to other stages. You will need to constantly be on your guard at the "look" stage, approaching each pericope as if it were the only one in the Bible and with no preconceptions of your own. As you write down your findings, ask yourself, "Is this a fact based on the text?"

Listen

And then it is time to "listen" to what you have found in the observation phase. This is the "compiling" aspect of inductive study, by which you attempt to tie together your findings into a cohesive "story" that makes sense based on the passage.

But this step involves far more than compiling facts. You have taken the story apart and looked at the facts as almost separate entities; now you will want to re-create the story for yourself, almost as if you had come upon the passage's original context as a bystander. For completing this step, the following three ideas are useful.

1. Sticking with the facts, begin to pull together your observations in order to make sense of your findings. Combining a few observations from Philemon 12-16 yields the following:

Philemon 12-16: Compiled Observations

  a. There are three characters in the story: the author, a slave and a slave owner.

  b. The author is preparing the slave owner for the return of his slave, from whom he had been separated for a little while.

  c. The slave has become a believer in Christ.

  d. The author is very close to the slave and to the slave owner . . . etc.

2. As the ideas come together, categorize them under the following cate-

gories: who, where, when and what (sound familiar?). You will discover that every observation made in the "look" stage will answer one of the four questions. Categorizing observations in Philemon yields the following.

Who: Three characters—the author, who is in chains; the slave, a new believer in Christ who is returning to his owner; and the slave owner, who is a friend of the author. The slave is now considered a brother in Christ to his owner.

Where: The author is in chains, therefore in prison.

When: The events occurred while the author was in chains, and the slave and owner were separated for "a little while."

What: The slave is very precious to the author; the slave was helpful to the spread of the gospel; the author wanted to be sensitive to the wishes and motivations of the slave owner; the slave is perceived by the author as no longer a slave to the owner but a brother in Christ, and possibly a deeper brother in Christ than to the author himself; a possible reason the slave and owner were separated was so that they could be reunited under the best possible circumstances.

3. Then, re-create the facts in such a way that you can subjectively identify with their reality. This is where "listening" comes in. Perhaps you put the story together based on the information given, but felt nothing. Now you can utilize the senses—seeing, hearing, touching, feeling, smelling and tasting. And this is where you begin the transition from observation to interpretation.

Imagine the ambivalence of a slave returning to his master, no longer as a slave but now as a brother. Feel the tears the author must have shed when he said goodby to the slave and wrote these words. Put yourselves into the skin of the slave traveling hot and dusty roads, leaving one who had empowered him for another who had the legal right to exercise complete power over him. Identify with the tension the slave owner may have felt when reading this letter, borne by his slave, in which he was being entreated to treat the slave as a brother in Christ rather than as a slave.

As you learn to put "color" onto black-and-white factual images, you will begin to relive the events and teachings of God's Word in such a way that they make sense *because you are experiencing them.* This is where Bible study gets exciting! The Bible is a book about *relationships,* and it is based upon human-divine *experience,* so Bible students must learn to use their God-given senses through imagination. Utilizing your senses will allow the Bible to come alive, and your life will never be the same.

Just think about sitting in a tree on a hot day waiting for Jesus to pass, only to have him stop and invite himself to your home, and you start understanding why Zacchaeus was touched so deeply and responded so readily. Become the man named Peter meeting the Master on a strip of sand. Sniff the fish being cooked over a small fire in the early morning, listen to the waves lap gently upon the shore as you converse with Jesus, and you will never forget the forgiveness of Christ that looks beyond even desertion and denial. The Bible is waiting to be explored, and observation allows you to begin the process in an accurate yet creative way.

Pulling Things Together

Are you ready to do your own work? You will make observations on Malachi 2:17—3:5 under the two categories "look" and "listen"; since the passage has already been chosen for you, the "stop" stage has been taken care of.

Just as my students were freed to praise God when they stopped and observed a simple flower, so you will fall in love with God's Word if you take the time to get the facts and then experience them. Malachi 2:17—3:5 is rich with facts, color and passion. Like a detective, search this passage, and let the Master himself speak!

Personal Study and Reflection

1. Begin a new page in your Malachi workbook. At the top left corner put "Look!" Then leave a large space and farther down in the page put "Listen!"

2. Under "Look!" make as many observations on Malachi 2:17—3:5 as you are able. Try to make at least twenty. Remember, an observation is based on this passage alone.

3. Under "Listen!" sort the observations found through observation into the categories "who," "where," "when," "what." Each observation written at the top of the page will fit under one of these categories.

Digging Deeper in Group Study

1. Discuss: As a group pull out your notebooks and, if possible, go verse by verse through Malachi 2:17—3:5. Let each member list his or her observations.

2. Interactive exercise: Spend some time "listening" to this passage. It contains vivid, colorful imagery. As a group write down the images that this passage employs (example: "God is 'wearied' ").

After making a list, discuss the images together. Use your senses; talk about experiences that can help make the word pictures come alive (for instance, has anyone in the group ever seen a silversmith at work?).

5

ASKING
INTERPRETIVE
QUESTIONS

I magine digging back through the archives of your family history. While searching through genealogical lists and dusty back rooms of libraries you come across the following document, perhaps written by one of your relatives:

It was obvious to all that she was unusual when she was still a little girl. Her talent for music was incomprehensible, given the lack of musical ability in the family. Everything she has tried—composing; playing the piano, violin, harpsichord, and flute; and even conducting—has turned to gold. So you can understand our excitement over this opportunity to study with the greatest master of our time, T . . .

How would you feel after reading such a document? What kinds of questions would be going through your thoughts? Surely they would be questions such as these: Is this written by a relative? When was it written? Is the girl a relative? Who is the great master? Where did she study? Was she famous? Why does the note end abruptly?

The one thing you know for sure after reading this document is that it raises more questions than it answers. It is incomplete. And given the possibility that you have a famous relative, you will probably begin the inductive process in order to get more information.

So making use of what you learned about observation in chapter four, you come up with the following: There is a girl; she is perceived by the author as a musical genius; she has been successful at composing, playing various instruments and conducting; she will be/is studying with a person perceived by the author as the greatest master of the time the note was written; the author and others are excited about the possibilities.

With these facts in hand, you have ideas that can be explored. Like a detective "hot on the trail" of a suspect, you have enough information to begin probing in greater detail. But where do you start? How can you possibly find the information necessary to help you understand the time-worn note?

Welcome to Interpretation!
In order to learn more, you need to move to step two of the inductive process. That step is _interpretation_. You will notice that simply observing has given you only part of the information that you need. The small scrap of paper you hold leaves many questions unanswered. You need to start looking elsewhere for answers.

There is potentially no limit to your search. Beginning with a careful examination of the box in which you located the scrap, your quest for information could take you to universities, to elderly friends of your family, to music historians. You may choose to have a professional "date" your note so that you get a general sense of the time period in which the note was written. Then you can search for all master musicians of that era whose names begin with the letter *T*. You can try to correlate the data with what you know about where your family was located at certain times.

If you have the interest and dogged persistence to learn, you will eventually begin to uncover more clues and will be better able to make sense of your findings.

Welcome to interpretation! Moving beyond the limited facts contained in a text, your role at this stage is to interact with the facts, then to search through an ever-widening circle, beginning with the immediate context, for answers. You will have completed this step when all the necessary information has been located—information that will help you to understand a particular text and respond to what you have found.

You may be wondering what kinds of questions need to be answered. How do you know what to look for and where to go as you interact with your observations and attempt to complete the picture begun with the observation stage? In the next sections we will discuss what questions to ask and where to go when interpreting the Bible.

The Logical Flow

The inductive process is beautiful in its simplicity. Thus you will not be surprised to know that the same questions you ask in the interpretation stage are the ones you've already learned to ask in book study and in the observation stage. In inductive study, the who, where, when, what and why questions *must* be answered as completely as possible before appropriate application can be made. So the purpose of both the observation and interpretation stages is to help you work through these questions systematically.

The difference between observation and interpretation is that in observation you must stay within the boundaries of a particular pericope, while in interpretation the surrounding context—indeed, the whole Bible and more—is fair game. In observation, you act as a bystander coming upon a scene, attempting to piece together the facts. In interpretation, you become a probing detective attempting to dig even deeper to make sense of your findings.

Your job in interpretation is threefold: first, to fill in the gaps of the who, when, where and what questions not directly answered by the text in the observation stage; second, to arrive at a logical conclusion regarding the author's main intent ("why"); and third, to understand how the structure of the passage supports the author's intent (the "how," which is the subject of chapter six). So you can see the logical flow of the interpretation stage: from historical context (who, where, when) to ideas presented (what) to author's main intent (why) to outline of thought flow (how).

Step 1: Complete Who, When, Where and What Questions

The first step in the interpretation stage is merely a continuation of the observation stage. Your task is to take the who, when, where and what questions and answer them as completely as possible by utilizing all the tools at your disposal.

Following is a brief outline of questions you will seek to answer (note the similarities between this outline and the outline given for study of a Bible book):

Who
Author: mindset, circumstances
Recipients: relationship to author, direct/indirect references from the passage
Characters: all "players," whether directly or indirectly mentioned
Where
All places mentioned and their characteristics; descriptions of places and events
When
Time of writing, any times mentioned in the passage, time span of events

What
Ideas or themes that are repeated, emphasized, easily discovered
Problems or circumstances addressed by the author
Theological words whose meanings have a bearing on the passage

When answering the questions from the above outline, you are free to work from within and outside the passage you are studying. The work you've already done is a resource, but there are others as well. Follow these steps:

1. *Review your findings from the observation step.* There is no need to duplicate the work you've already done. In your inductive study notebook, create a new page(s) for the interpretation step with the basic outline from above, spaced in such a way that you can fill in the blanks. Then go back to the observations you made as you worked through chapter four and write your findings in the outline.

2. *Review work done earlier in the book you are studying as well as your book-overview findings.* In addition to using your observations on the passage, you can turn to the work you did when you prepared for inductive study of the book by doing an overview (the subject of chapters two and three). Relevant information from this work can be added to the outline.

3. *Use immediate context when interpreting passages.* As you will no doubt discover, the work and observation you've already done will not answer every question you have about a particular passage. So you next look in the passages surrounding your pericope for answers and clues. This will be especially necessary when the passage alludes to historical events or concepts and theological ideas that are not necessarily bound strictly to the passage you are studying. A Reformation saying is applicable in such cases: "Let Scripture interpret Scripture." By tracing theological and practical ideas through larger sections of a book you allow the Bible to inform your study.

4. *Apply other tools as necessary, including other books of the Bible, concordances, Bible dictionaries and Bible wordbooks.* Remember, your scope of study in the interpretation step is potentially unlimited. There are thousands of

resources you may learn to consult, but in inductive study concordances, dictionaries and wordbooks will prove helpful.

Suppose you want to understand the Philippian people in order to make sense of the letter to the Philippians. After beginning your study with Philippians itself, your study can move on to Acts (which includes the story of how the church in Philippi came into being), other epistles of Paul and then a Bible dictionary for maps and a description of Philippi in Paul's time. Such a course of study will yield some extremely helpful information that will enable you to better understand the recipients of Paul's letter.

If you are able to summarize "who," "when," "where" and "what," you have completed a time-consuming yet necessary part of inductive study. Spend as much effort as is necessary on your summaries, since the four sentences are the result of all your work to the present time, from observation through interpretation.

To show you how this works with the book of Philemon, we again turn to Philemon 12-16. You can look back to chapter four to refresh yourself on the observations that we made on this passage. Now, as our research scope increases, we can gather all the facts and boil them down into one-sentence summaries.

Before you read this section, it may be helpful to attempt to do it yourself and then check your findings against mine.

Who: Paul (along with Timothy), Philemon and Onesimus. Onesimus is a new believer in Christ, the slave of Philemon and a dear friend and helper of Paul. _Summary:_ Paul wrote to Philemon about Onesimus, who was Philemon's slave.

When: Paul was in prison. Since the letter mentions Epaphras from the church in Colosse, it may be that Philemon was written about the same time as Colossians. The letter was written after Onesimus had become a Christian. _Summary:_ This letter was written while Paul was in prison, after he had led Onesimus to Christ and discipled him in the faith, on the occasion of Onesimus's return to Philemon.

Where: Paul was perhaps in Rome and Philemon in Colosse; Onesimus had to travel to return to his master. *Summary:* Paul wrote Philemon from Rome, while Onesimus traveled to Colosse, Philemon's residence.

What: After a somewhat lengthy, and perhaps flattering, introduction, Paul seems to get to the heart of his purpose in these verses. Ideas include the fact that Paul was sending Onesimus home (implying that Onesimus needed a "nudge"); Paul was in chains for the furthering of the gospel; Onesimus was Paul's "very heart," extremely dear and helpful to him, as opposed to Onesimus's former uselessness to Philemon; Paul wanted Philemon's response to be spontaneous; Paul emphasizes that Onesimus is now Philemon's brother in Christ rather than a slave. *Summary:* Paul wanted Philemon to accept Onesimus as a brother in Christ, and to that end he attempted to offer persuasive reasons that Philemon would benefit from accepting Onesimus.

Step 2: Write a One-Sentence Purpose Statement

You are now ready to move to the all-important "purpose statement." You will notice that we are not breaking new ground, since you learned about developing a purpose statement (for a whole book of the Bible) in chapter three.

Simply stated, the purpose statement attempts to pull together the historical context and issues being addressed in a comprehensive manner that clearly states what the author intended the original readers to understand. To put this into an equation:

Historical Context (Who/When/Where) + Ideas/Themes (What) =
Author's Purpose (Why)

For example, after reading a book explaining tennis you would say that the author intended for the reader to better understand the game of tennis. Within the book there will be a number of emphases that, upon inductive examination, can yield various other purpose statements. A particular chapter may elaborate on different aspects of net play. A section in that chapter may have the purpose of teaching about forehand net play—and so on. A purpose statement for each unit can enable the student to keep moving in the direction intended by the author.

You will most likely find that developing a purpose statement for a Bible passage is more difficult than writing one for a tennis manual. That is because the Bible uses many literary genres, including poetry, prophecy, letters and historical chronicles, to convey its ideas.

Compiling the information gathered on Philemon 12-16, what would you say Paul's intent was in writing this section of Scripture?

Here is a possibility:

Paul wrote Philemon from prison on the occasion of the return of Onesimus (Philemon's slave), in order to prepare Philemon to receive Onesimus as an equal based on the fact that Onesimus had found Christ, was a true brother in the faith and was loved by Paul.

The author's intent, the "why," is critical if you want to study the Bible over the long term. It is the focal point of the first two steps, observation and interpretation, and it is the only "door" into correct application. So all your hard work to this point pays off when you develop an accurate statement of author's intent.

Step 3: Test Purpose Statement by Outlining Passage

Once you have developed a purpose statement, you can test it against the passage you are studying to make sure that it works. This is where outlining and structural analysis enter the picture. We will discuss both topics in chapter six.

Who Was "T"?

Remember our example from the beginning of the chapter? As you dug and researched, leaving no stones unturned, you began to uncover some amazing clues. When all the information had been amassed and you were able to answer "who," "where," "when" and "what," you discovered that the author was thrilled that his daughter, Tricia (your great-great-grandmother, by the way), had gone to study with the great musician Tchaikovsky! Imagine, a member of your family studying with one of the all-time greats!

Wouldn't it be worth all the time and effort you had lavished on learning more about your relative? Of course. In the same way, the Bible is waiting to reward those who will pay the price of careful study.

Now you will continue to study Malachi, attempting to "boil down" Malachi 2:17—3:5 into a clear and comprehensive statement of author's intent.

Personal Study and Reflection

1. Begin a new page in your notebook. Arrange this outline on the paper, or create your own outline.

Step 1: Compiling Answers

Who:

Where:

When:

What:

Step 2: One-Sentence Summaries

Who:

Where:

When:

What:

Summary of Author's Intent (Why):

2. Now, turn back to Malachi 2:17—3:5 and fill in the worksheet, following the steps this chapter has outlined. Your purpose is to develop an accurate statement of author's intent.

Digging Deeper in Group Study

1. Discuss: What were some of the resources outside of Malachi that group members used, and how effective were they at helping to answer the questions in the personal study time?

2. Interactive exercise: To reinforce the students' individual work, spend group time doing interpretive work. The following steps will be helpful.

a. List the questions that need to be answered from outside the text. Don't worry about the answers, even if individuals have them. Just come up with the questions.

b. Using whatever resources are available, including the students' work, begin to answer as many questions as possible.

c. Develop a group statement of author's intent.

Then discuss: How does this statement compare with the individual ones?

How has working as a group allowed you to develop a more accurate statement?

6

DISCOVERING A **P**ASSAGE'S **S**TRUCTURE

*T*he building towered majestically over the smaller high-rises that rose across the skyline. As I walked about the lookout area on the top floor, I was overwhelmed with feelings of awe. You could see for miles! People looked like tiny fleas dotting the streets below, while cars drove antlike through an endless figure-eight pattern of highways. Faraway landmarks, which appeared near as time and space, were given a new dimension.

The most amazing feeling, however, was wondering at the intelligence required to build such an edifice. Tall and narrow, it seemed at a distance as if a strong wind could blow it over. Yet inside, even at the top, there was a feeling of strength and stability. How had the architects and builders done it? What did they know that enabled them to confidently place this building in the city's skyline? One thing was certain—I cared less for the beauty of the building than I did for its stability!

An architect would want to show me the building's structure to reassure me. It is the structure, from foundation through pinnacle, that allows the building to stand through sun, snow and even hurricanes. Steel girders and bolts hold the building securely underneath the painted panels that make the rooms attractive. The fact that there are local, state and federal requirements for structural integrity shows that a solid structure is essential for a building of any kind.

Structural Analysis in Bible Study

Structure is no less important in written communication. Whether you know it or not, whenever you read a book, a sign or a paragraph, you engage in *structural analysis*. This means that you are attempting to sift through words and word order in order to capture core truths and supporting statements. Every person able to read operates on this level.

And we have arrived at this point in inductive Bible study—perhaps the most challenging part of all. Having taken apart a passage through observation, then examined it and discovered its core truth through the first two steps of interpretation, we are now ready to put it back together through outlining and structural analysis (the third step of interpretation).

This part of inductive study will likely seem difficult and awkward at first. Yet it provides an exciting dimension of Bible study. Having already discovered the core truth in a passage through the previous steps, you now get to see how the whole passage has been constructed to support and reinforce that main idea.

In this chapter you'll do a very detailed study of the structure of a passage. You'll be relieved to know that you will probably not have to study Scripture in such detail for the rest of your life! But you'll find that understanding a passage's *structure* can contribute to your understanding of its *meaning*.

There are at least two good reasons that structural analysis is difficult to grasp. First, we are not trained in principles of logic, which, among other things, allow us to understand relationships, sequences and interrelationships. Not many of us have taken courses in logic, and certainly few are able instinctively to implement logical reasoning in Bible study.

The second reason structural analysis is difficult is that there is a tendency in the church to do what is called *proof-texting*—searching the Bible to support our own ideas instead of working carefully through whole books and allowing God's Word to dictate our response. Pastors and teachers, who are constantly under pressure to come up with ideas for sermons and lessons, are especially likely to resort to proof-texting. It's tempting to develop an idea and then seek passages that support the idea rather than coming upon passages and using their structure to dictate the sermon or lesson structure.

One result of this way of preaching and teaching is that people in the pews tend to miss the connection between a sermon and the text on which it is supposed to be based. The subtle message is that the Bible is used as a takeoff point for sermons and lessons. And since most people do not feel comfortable enough with their own training and knowledge, they may feel inadequate when using the Bible because they don't see what the pastor or teacher seems to be seeing in a text.

Structural analysis, properly applied, will enable the Bible student to read the Word of God free from presuppositions that lead to proof-texting; the result will be greater insight and integrity in Bible study, and your mind will be opened to a tremendous storehouse of knowledge that might otherwise have been missed.

What Is Structural Analysis?

The term *structural analysis* is probably enough to strike fear in the heart of even the most courageous Bible student. It is an imposing term that requires definition.

There are two parts to structural analysis. First, there is the element of *structure,* in which a passage is carefully outlined to support its core idea. Then comes the *analysis,* when the outline is studied in greater detail in order to note, among other things, repeated words and phrases and the interrelationships of words and phrases. *In structural analysis, the Bible student carefully outlines a passage around its core idea and then studies the outline intently in order to derive maximum benefit.*

Learning to Outline

The first part of structural analysis is to carefully prepare an outline of the text being studied. You can do that by following the following steps. We will continue our study of Philemon 12-16 as we move through the process.

1. Outline a passage using the exact words of the passage. This helps in two ways. First, it relieves you of the pressure of needing to paraphrase and condense. And second, it maintains the integrity of the biblical text.

2. Use and refine your purpose statement as you work through the passage. When you developed a purpose statement for the passage, you sought to isolate the one main thought that is being conveyed (what I term the "subject, verb and direct object" below). As you start to outline, then, you can use your purpose statement for direction. If your purpose statement ends up not totally fitting the passage by the time you are done outlining, then you can redo it to make it relevant again. You will remember from chapter five our statement of author's intent for Philemon 12-16:

> Paul wrote Philemon from prison on the occasion of the return of Onesimus (Philemon's slave), in order to prepare Philemon to receive Onesimus as an equal based on the fact that Onesimus had found Christ, was a true brother in the faith and was loved by Paul.

3. Follow the rules of English grammar to the best of your ability. Do you remember analyzing sentences in high-school or college English class? It can be tedious and demanding, but principles of grammar can help you understand the meaning behind complex sentences and paragraphs.

We will not spend a great deal of time going over what can be learned in high-school English, even though many may have forgotten (this is a good time to brush up on your English!), but several elements are important to identify in the sentence or paragraph you are outlining.

Find all verbs and verb forms. The easiest type of word to identify, and the one most helpful for outlining, is the verb. Sentences are built around action, and verbs are words of "action or state of being." Anything that denotes action should be found and put on a list.

You may want to stop for a moment and underline all verbs and verb forms in Philemon 12-16:

> I am sending him—who is my very heart—back to you. I would have liked to keep him with me so that he could take your place in helping me while I am in chains for the gospel. But I did not want to do anything without your consent, so that any favor you do will be spontaneous and not forced. Perhaps the reason he was separated from you for a little while was that you might have him back for good—no longer as a slave, but better than a slave, as a dear brother. He is very dear to me but even dearer to you, both as a man and as a brother in the Lord.

Find the subject, main verb and direct object. You remember these—the "Big Three" of English. When you first learned to read you were presented with sentences like "Jack threw the ball" and "Mary rode the bicycle." In the first sentence, "Jack" is the subject, "threw" is the main verb and "ball" is the direct object. As you recall, the subject is the one performing the action; the main verb is the primary action performed by the subject; and the direct object is the recipient/object of the subject's action.

Locating the subject, verb and direct object is a little more complicated in complex sentences and paragraphs, for you have to know enough English grammar to work through the smokescreen of modifying words, clauses and verb forms. Remember, too, that every full sentence must have a subject and a main verb, but not every sentence has an object.

Look at Philemon 12-16, and see if you can locate a key sentence with a primary subject, verb and direct object for the whole section. A hint: One short sentence dictates the content of the modifying sentences and phrases that follow.

Seeking the primary phrase, you could conceivably choose "I would have liked to keep him," with "I" being the subject, "would have liked to keep" the verb phrase and "him" the direct object. But then when you try to place verse 12 ("I am sending him") as a modifying phrase, it does not make sense.

Instead, the topic sentence of verses 12-16 is this: "I am sending him." You can scan the rest of the passage and see that the remaining words and phrases modify and explain this simple phrase.

Main phrase: I am sending him

☐ who is my very heart

☐ I would have liked to keep him with me

☐ I did not want to do anything without your consent

☐ perhaps the reason he was separated from you for a little while

Notice that if you had chosen any of the other (supporting) phrases, you would have not been able to arrange the passage as neatly as I have done.

Construct "sentences within sentences." Your next step is to work on the different supporting clauses to isolate mini-sentences as well. Within Philemon 12-16, there are eleven of these mini-sentences. Can you locate them?

Here they are:

☐ who is my very heart

☐ I would have liked to keep him

☐ he could take your place

☐ I am in chains

☐ I did not want to do anything

☐ any favor you do will be spontaneous and not forced

☐ the reason . . . was . . .

☐ he was separated from you

☐ you might have him

☐ he is very dear to me

☐ (he is) even dearer to you

☐ he is very dear to me

☐ (he is) even dearer to you

Place modifiers (adjectives and adverbs) under (or next to) the words that they modify. As you continue to break the sentence down, the next logical step is to find what are known as *modifiers:* words that further describe other words and phrases. It is helpful to take the eleven phrases from above and fit the appropriate adjectives and adverbs under them. So, for instance, your work would yield:

who is heart

    my

    very

My and *very* help to explain *heart* in this instance. Take a moment and fit other modifiers into the ten remaining mini-sentences. While you work, ask: Does this word help explain the word it is placed under?

Finally, put phrases under the words/phrases that they modify. The last step in working with outlining is to logically connect the sentences in such a way that the main subject, verb and direct object are supported by the surrounding clauses that modify them. A modifying phrase is a phrase or mini-sentence that expounds upon an idea, word or phrase.

So, for instance, "he could take your place" modifies "would have liked to keep him," with "so that" as the connecting words. In outline it looks something like this:

would have liked to keep him

      so that he could take your place

In Philemon 12-16, the rest of the passage builds upon the fact that Paul is sending Onesimus to Philemon. Before you look over my outline, which appears below, you may want to follow the steps above to create your own.

On your outline, place subordinate, modifying clauses and words beneath and to the right of words and phrases they actually modify. Second, put matching or parallel verbs and phrases in some sort of alignment—vertical or horizontal—to show their connection (example: "He is dear to me" is placed directly over "[he is] even dearer to you").

Here is a hint for working with an outline like this. It helps to think out loud. Things often sound more logical, or illogical, when spoken than they do when merely thought in our minds.

Analysis of Outline

Once you have constructed an outline, it is time to analyze it for clues that will shed even more light on the text. This is where analysis comes in. In structural analysis you identify interrelationships between words and phrases. Here are some of the relationships you need to look for.

☐ Comparison: association of similar things or ideas ("white as wool")

☐ Contrast: association of opposite things or ideas ("black and white")

☐ Repetition: reiteration of ideas or words ("Jesus wept"; "he cried bitterly")

☐ Cause to effect: statement of a cause and its effect ("sin leads to death")

☐ Effect to cause: cause and effect stated in reverse order ("crashes come from improper driving")

☐ Explanation: expansion of an idea ("Emmanuel, which means 'God with us' ")

☐ Illustration: example given to enhance an idea (". . . is like a sower, who went forth . . .")

☐ Climax: high point of a story or discourse ("All this was written so that you may believe . . .")

☐ Pivot: point in text or story where change in direction occurs ("Suddenly, a thin wiry man came blasting through the door")

☐ Interchange: movement back and forth between ideas ("Going back to our original thesis . . .")

☐ Preparation: inclusion of background information to provide the setting for what is to follow ("This having been said, we can now proceed with our story")

☐ Question posed: basing a text around certain questions ("What shall we say then—shall we go on sinning that grace may abound?")

☐ Question answered: basing a text on answers provided to questions, stated or implied ("You want to know why I hid for three weeks? First . . .")

☐ Main thought: main idea around which text revolves

The way analysis works is simple. After carefully outlining a passage on paper, you take several colored pencils or pens and make notations on your outline when you locate any of the literary devices listed above.

Try it with Philemon 12-16. Here is my attempt:

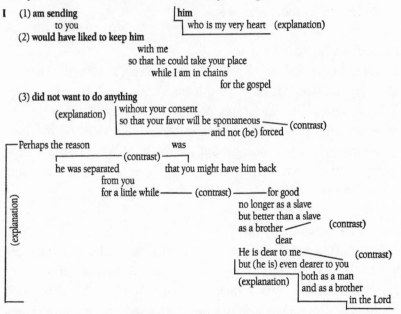

Once you have done an analysis you can start to draw conclusions about the text. In Philemon 12-16 we should note Paul's use of contrast. Locate the five contrasts in the second half of the passage (he—you, separated—have him back, a slave—better than a slave, a slave—a brother, dear to me—even dearer to you). Paul appears to be using this set of contrasts for the purpose of emphasizing the depth of relationship Onesimus would have with Philemon.

For Your Practice
You may be feeling like the man who wants to build a large, beautiful home but is overcome with anxiety and dread as he stands on his undeveloped lot with shovel and hammer in hand. Structural analysis is challenging, but it's also full of rewards. You will discover that for yourself after outlining and analyzing Malachi 2:17—3:5. Structural analysis is an exciting part of inductive study, and although it may not come easily to you at first, it is worth the time for those who persist.

Personal Study and Reflection
1. At the top of a sheet of paper in your notebook, write the purpose statement (the "why") from your previous study.
2. Then, working as carefully as possible and taking as much time as necessary, attempt to do an outline of Malachi 2:17—3:5 (if you have trouble, try outlining a smaller portion, such as 2:17—3:1). Follow the steps given in this chapter. If you are completely stumped, consult the outline in appendix two.

Digging Deeper in Group Study
1. Discuss: How did each of you do, and feel, as you outlined the passage? What little tricks did each person find to figure out the structure?
2. Discuss: Come up with a group outline (use a large piece of paper or overhead projector, if available), using the work individuals prepared during the week.
3. Interactive exercise: Now do a structural analysis together, using the categories found in this chapter. Discuss what the analysis helps you to discover.

7

MAKING
APPROPRIATE
APPLICATION

There was a man who came to see Jesus at night: Nicodemus the Pharisee, a member of the Jewish ruling council. The story of his visit with Jesus is told in John 3. In this passage we meet a man who had status, a good name and money. Interested in Jesus but not wanting to sacrifice the benefits his religion had brought him, he sought Jesus at night, hoping that his Jesus-hating friends would not find out.

Jesus was quite willing to talk with Nicodemus, but not to accommodate his fears. In the course of their conversation, documented by John, he proceeded to tell his religious friend that he (Christ) was the only way to salvation, that those who chose to follow would be saved, and that those who rejected him would perish.

Then Jesus told Nicodemus something very interesting, in verses 19-21:

"This is the verdict: Light has come into the world, but men loved darkness instead of light because their deeds were evil. Everyone who does evil hates the light, and will not come into the light for fear that his deeds will be exposed. But whoever lives by the truth comes into the light, so that it may be seen plainly that what he has done has been done through God."

What was Jesus saying? I believe he was making a number of important statements to Nicodemus, including these:

☐ You came at night because you are scared to show others your true feelings, so you are in the dark.

☐ I, Jesus, am light, exposing what happens in the dark and inviting people to come into the light.

☐ Those who live by truth are not scared of the light, because they have the approval of God.

☐ Most people willingly choose darkness because they prefer to remain evil.

Jesus was challenging Nicodemus. As a Pharisee, Nicodemus had been trained in the Law to walk in God's way. He had learned how to be a good person. He was no doubt greatly respected and accorded the status of a community leader. Yet Jesus exhorted him to throw away the cloak of respectability, which he so desperately wanted to keep, for the garment of righteousness that comes from walking in God's light.

Jesus wanted Nicodemus to see the Light, who is Jesus, and to respond by accepting the life-giving and direction-providing qualities of that Light. Jesus is called "the Light" in John—not "*a* light" or "another bright spot on the horizon," but "*the* Light." Without light, there is no life (consider what would happen to our world without the sun), and in the absence of light there is no direction. Christ gives both. Christ *is* both.

Making the Connection
You may be wondering how the story of Nicodemus fits into a chapter on

application. Here is the point: Like Nicodemus, you may be a Bible scholar, church leader or average church member who knows a great deal *about* the Bible, but you can still miss the message *of* the Bible. One who claims to walk in the Light may still be stumbling about in the darkness of pride and desires to dominate others.

Instead of using the Bible as "a lamp to our feet and a light to our path" (see Ps 119:105), we can just as easily use it as a bludgeon (to beat others into submission); a platform (to further our own agenda); a medal of honor (to build up the ego); or an interesting novel (to read for information and stories). Inductive Bible study has these dangers. We can have so much fun digging around in the Bible text, noting subtle interrelationships and discovering great theological truths, that we forget to open the "treasure chest" of God's Word to see how it can, indeed must, affect our own lives. It's like walking into a room full of light switches, enjoying the challenge of locating each one, then forgetting to turn them on.

That is why there are two chapters in this manual on applying scriptural truths to your life. According to John, "The Word became flesh and made his dwelling among us" (Jn 1:14). In Christ, God's Living Word, we confront a person who demands a response. It may be easy to dodge facts written on the Bible's pages, but to evade a living person (Christ) is impossible.

So we come to application, in which we learn how to take all that has been learned in a passage and make it relevant to our individual lives. All previous study in this book, including our study in Philemon and Malachi, has led to this crucial point. It is where "the rubber meets the road," but only if you are ready to ask some probing questions of yourself.

There are three basic steps to application. First, you ask how the original readers (and participants) were expected to respond to the information provided in the text; then, you put yourself into the shoes of the readers (and participants); and finally you decide on a course of action in response to what you have learned.

What Was Expected of Them?

The purpose statement, in combination with the outline you learned to develop in chapter six, is the key to application. But the purpose statement does not necessarily state what was expected of the original readers. It is simply an inductive study vehicle to communicate the core idea that the author wanted to present. The actual response that came as a result of the Word applied is usually one step further, discovered when you apply the following few principles.

1. *Use your God-given logic to combine all that you have learned from a particular passage into a clear, comprehensive application for the original readers/participants.*

To show how this works we will continue working with Philemon 12-16:

> I am sending him—who is my very heart—back to you. I would have liked to keep him with me so that he could take your place in helping me while I am in chains for the gospel. But I did not want to do anything without your consent, so that any favor you do will be spontaneous and not forced. Perhaps the reason he was separated from you for a little while was that you might have him back for good—no longer as a slave, but better than a slave, as a dear brother. He is very dear to me but even dearer to you, both as a man and as a brother in the Lord.

Working with this text in the past few chapters we have made observations, developed a statement of purpose ("Paul wrote Philemon from prison on the occasion of the return of Onesimus (Philemon's slave), in order to prepare Philemon to receive Onesimus as an equal based on the fact that Onesimus had found Christ, was a true brother in the faith and was loved by Paul") and performed a structural analysis on the text. Out of our study came many interesting clues, not the least of which was the repeated use of contrast (as you recall, five times in these verses) by Paul, seemingly to provide a subtle lesson about the ability of a person to change from evil to good.

Stop now, and before reading what follows, look over the passage and try to come up with your own statement of application. Here are my own thoughts.

There are a number of things about this passage that must have at least caught Philemon's attention. Paul went out of his way to show Philemon the depth of his love for Onesimus, calling him "my very heart" and saying, "I would like to keep him with me" and "He is very dear to me." In addition, Paul made liberal use of contrast in the final few verses, the most obvious one being the contrast between a slave and a brother. This repeated use of contrast gives passion and color to Paul's words.

There were several reasons he would have spoken so highly of Onesimus. First, there had been a marked change in Onesimus based on his contact with Paul and with Jesus Christ. Second, according to Paul, Onesimus had been useless to Philemon before (some think he may have run away and even stolen from his master). Since Onesimus was a slave, Philemon would probably tend to look down on him, and Paul didn't want that. Third, as a Christian Onesimus was, indeed, Philemon's brother in Christ. His coming home was initiated through his contact with Paul and the need for reconciliation with those he may have hurt. Philemon needed to be prepared to forgive, love and empower. Fourth, Paul subtly implied that Onesimus must no longer be a slave to Philemon, but a trusted brother. Imagine the contrast between a trouble-making slave and a loving brother! This passage indeed shows the kind of change that is possible through a relationship with Jesus Christ.

There seems to be something more in this passage than a challenge for Philemon to receive Onesimus as a reconciled brother. The fact that someone becomes a Christian doesn't mean that he is worthy of great trust; the process of growth in Christ is in itself a slow and difficult road. Would Onesimus have undergone a radical, instantaneous change just through meeting Christ? Perhaps, because it is possible. But I believe that, once he had been touched by Christ, he grew significantly through his contact with Paul.

Imagine growing up a slave, having no rights and being used solely to meet the needs of others. Maybe Philemon the master was a loving exception, but the fact is that Onesimus had been a slave, and perhaps a rebellious one. He could have harbored all sorts of bitterness toward his master(s), and this didn't necessarily leave him at conversion. Many Christians still struggle with forgiveness after years of walking with Christ. If I were to put myself in his shoes, I would say that it would be terrifying to go home and once again place myself at the mercy of a master who had absolute authority over me. My ego would cry out against this, perhaps remembering punishments that had been inflicted in the past. Why not live in Rome and enjoy my newfound freedom (both in Christ and in life itself)? It would make more sense.

Of this I can speak with assurance: Onesimus was going home only after the conviction of the Holy Spirit and/or the prodding of Paul. I believe that God used Paul to direct Onesimus home. And this says something about Paul's relationship with Onesimus, as well as the lesson that Philemon was to learn from Paul. By choosing the phrases "my very heart" and "dear to me" to describe Onesimus, Paul was hoping to influence Philemon to treat Onesimus well; but he was also simply speaking truth. Paul had met Onesimus and led him to Christ. But he hadn't stopped there. He had loved Onesimus and had nurtured this young man in the faith until he was prepared to go home and face the future with his head held high. Paul saw worth in him, something that nobody else had probably ever seen, and he had found a way to lovingly draw him out until he blossomed like a rose. Then he encouraged the young man to take the greatest risk of his life: to face his master with nothing but a changed heart and a letter from his mentor.

Just think of the implications for racism and prejudice that are in this short book! Paul tells Philemon to accept Onesimus as a brother, no longer as a slave—yet Onesimus had done nothing to earn his freedom. All he had done was to meet a man named Paul and a Savior named Jesus Christ, and they had empowered him and set him free in his faith.

As you can see, there are a number of potential applications when you look at the text in this way. First, and most obvious, Paul expected Philemon (and others in the church at Colosse who were to read this letter) to receive Onesimus. Then he wanted Philemon to accept Onesimus as a full brother in Christ, not a half-brother or a stepchild in the faith.

But the greatest lesson of all is found indirectly in this passage, in the person of Paul. By providing clues into his own dealings with Onesimus, he demonstrated to Philemon and the church at Colosse the meaning of unconditional love. Paul demonstrated his love by reaching out and sharing the most precious gift he had, Jesus Christ; investing his own life in Onesimus; empowering Onesimus by finding worth in him; and expecting great things of him, even to the extent of deciding that Onesimus had become strong enough to take the risk of seeking Philemon's forgiveness.

In response, Philemon should forgive and accept Onesimus as a brother in Christ, but—equally important—he must learn to see worth in people, minister to them in Christ's name and invest his life in them, nurturing them in Christ's love.

As you can see, some of my conclusions were based upon facts provided in the text and logical connections that can be made (for instance, why would Paul speak so highly of Onesimus unless he had spent a great deal of time nurturing him?). Others came from clues in other parts of Philemon (v. 10, for example, shows that Paul had led Onesimus to Christ). And still others came from seeming subtleties in the text and strong probabilities based on history and common sense (for instance, how many slaves, especially those called "useless," have good self-esteem?). As you will learn in the next chapter, understanding relationships and personalities will help you to interpret and apply the Bible more effectively.

2. Avoid pitfalls and be careful to limit your application to lessons learned in the passage being studied.

By now you may know that there is no hard and fast rule governing application. Although some may dispute this, the Bible is about relationships and therefore encompasses a vast diversity of situations and genres.

There are a number of different opinions about how to make Bible application, ranging from wooden literalism ("if Scripture says it, it must be true") to rampant liberalism ("somewhere in there is God's Word, and I hope to find it"). Both of these have problems, as do less extreme models. If we were consistent literalists we would still be sacrificing animals as the Israelites were commanded in the Old Testament, while if we embraced extreme liberalism we would be wasting our time writing or reading a manual on Bible study—few people are smart enough to locate the tidbits of Scripture that represent "God's Word."

For the sake of simplicity, there should be only one rule: *Taking the Bible in all seriousness as God's infallible Word, study with integrity to learn what original readers/participants were to do in response to what they were seeing and hearing.* And that is what you just did, if you completed a statement of application on Philemon 12-16.

If you follow the above principle with tenacity and care, you can learn what God expected of the original biblical protagonists, and what he expects of you today. Then you can avoid a number of pitfalls.

First, passages may deal with cultural specifications that may not necessarily represent the norm for all cultures. You must remember that the Bible was written for a specific people in specific circumstances at a specific time. There are cultural "commands" in the New Testament as well as the Old Testament, and sometimes it's hard to figure out whether or how they apply to us today. The best you can do is discover the *principles* underlying cultural commands. For example, if Paul's command for women to cover their heads in worship is still applicable, the vast majority of churches today are in error. But if this command was valid only for a certain cultural setting, is there some principle behind it that we can still learn from today?

Here is another example. In the book of Numbers, God gave specific commands to the Israelites as to how they should arrange their camp around the ark of the covenant (representing God's presence) as they traveled through the wilderness. Does that mean that we sin when we fail to travel in that way? Of course not, but we can travel with God in our midst in the same way that God intended when he specified how the Israelites should lay out their camp.

A second pitfall is that we can be misled by seemingly incomplete theological data in a text. For example, wisdom is defined one way in one text and differently in another text. Does that mean there is a discrepancy or disagreement? By no means. What it means is that one author has highlighted one aspect of wisdom and another has chosen a different perspective. Always use the complete Bible story to define theological concepts, never one passage out of context.

A third pitfall to avoid is the temptation to draw an application out of any and every text. Given the human limitations of each individual, certain passages will be especially difficult for you to apply to yourself. If you have worked hard and are still unable to find an application that makes sense, then consult a commentary or move on to another portion of Scripture. So long as you are trying to hear God's voice in Scripture and are not dodging personal issues, other parts of the Bible will speak loudly and clearly to your heart.

Fourth, don't read history and poetry in a literal, wooden fashion. This will lead to error. For example, the historical books document a great many human failings, and we are not called to imitate the biblical characters in every way (if your wife is not able to bear a child, should you have sex with another woman as Abraham did in Genesis?). These types of literature teach great truths, but we have to understand *how* they teach. Bible history presents the facts of history from a theological perspective, but it does not aim to judge every event or to teach that the lifestyles of the Hebrew leaders necessarily followed God's plan. Biblical poetry demonstrates the strengths, and frailties, of the human-divine relationship through song and wise sayings.

A fifth and final pitfall is looking for something that is not obviously present in a text. In the centuries after Christ a group of theologians and Bible scholars allegorized the Bible to try to make it tell several stories at once (for instance, the Israelites' crossing of the Jordan River was an allegory of a person's coming to faith in Christ). Debate on allegorical interpretation has continued to this day, but let's leave that debate to the experts. You and I will do well to stick with inductive study and look for the obvious, remembering that the Bible was written to ordinary men and women.

How Do I Fit In?

As you can see, discerning application for the original recipients of Scripture can be a difficult undertaking, so you will be glad to know that the next two steps are a little more straightforward. Actually, they are easy only for those with good self-knowledge.

In this step you picture yourself in the shoes of the recipients and/or participants by comparing yourself with each different person. Using the analogy from earlier in the chapter, you take the Scripture text and, for the first time, allow its light to fall on you.

For example, when you read a Gospel account it is possible to identify with a number of different people in each text: the original recipients, the disciples, the bystanders, the persons being healed, the Pharisees and others. Once you've asked, "How were they expected to respond to the Master?" you can move to finding points of contact with them by asking such questions as these:

☐ How am I arrogant like the Pharisees?

☐ How am I searching for meaning like the one who was healed?

☐ What would it take for my faith to match that of the one who was healed?

☐ How can I identify with the disciples as they stood by and watched?

These points of contact are important because they allow you to identify yourself with the strengths and character flaws of the participants and recipients of the biblical story. But this can be difficult and uncomfortable. Christians don't generally like to expose their weaknesses, or to identify with sinful people. We dress up in nice clothes on Sunday and put on our "nice voices" to demonstrate how *good* we are. This application step can undo all of that, especially when we're doing Bible study in a group. What if the other members find out that we struggle with gossip, or cheating, or anger, or bitterness?

Actually, chances are that they already know. And maybe, just maybe, they can help you if you let them.

I think of the first Alcoholics Anonymous meeting that I attended. I am not an alcoholic, but I went with a friend to a small support group of Christians from AA, and it was a liberating experience. In the AA tradition, every person began by saying, "Hi, I'm X, and I am an alcoholic." Some said that they struggled with drugs and other addictions as well. Then each person shared his or her particular struggles with emotions, addictions and circumstances. When each had finished talking, every other person in the group said, "Thank you, X."

I couldn't believe what I was hearing! People seated in a church were openly sharing their weaknesses and needs, and because of the accepting environment they felt free to work on their issues. Many AA members will tell you that their group is the first place they were truly accepted and loved.

We all are weak and needy in certain areas, and some of us run from what we know. Perhaps scared of what others will think, or maybe fearful to admit that part of our life is useless (sometimes a big part!), we allow lies to creep into our lives: "Yes, everything's fine; no, nothing's wrong." Jesus calls us to throw off our religious respectability and present ourselves before his Word, and each other, with humility.

That is what should happen at the present stage of Bible study. Instead of sitting in judgment on others or looking down on those presented in the text ("I'd never do that!"), we put ourselves in their place, trying to understand who they were and why they acted as they did. Then we can identify issues from our own lives that need to be addressed, issues God's Word is speaking to in the text.

In the case of Philemon, we have already isolated the application possibilities from verses 12-16. Again, here is my conclusion:

> In response, Philemon should forgive and accept Onesimus as a brother in Christ, but—equally important—he must learn to see worth in people, minister to them in Christ's name and invest his life in them, nurturing them in Christ's love.

Now, working from that simple application statement, isolate five questions you can ask of yourself—"do I?" "would I?" "how would I?" kinds of questions:

1.

2.

3.

4.

5.

Here are a few possibilities: Are there people that I need to forgive and accept, especially brothers and sisters in Christ? Would I respond positively if I received a similar letter from a friend about the need to forgive another? Do I see worth in all people? How effective am I at ministering to people in need? What does it mean to "nurture someone in Christ's love," and how am I a nurturing (or a nonnurturing) friend?

As you ask the questions, put yourself into the place of the Colossians, of Paul, of Philemon and of Onesimus. In doing so, you will learn much from God's Word.

What Is Expected of Me?

The third step involves acting as you feel God wants you to. This is the accountability step, in which you decide on a course of action and begin acting upon it. And it is here that a loving community becomes especially important.

It is difficult, sometimes even impossible, to grow unless we are involved in healthy, honest relationships (the subject of chapter ten). Left to your own devices, you would certainly ferret out some issues and growth needs that are addressed in the biblical text. But few people know themselves well enough to see all the issues in their lives that need work. How much of your body would you be able to see if you wanted to examine it with a flashlight? There are many places you cannot even see.

Others most likely see our growth needs better than we do, for our weaknesses come out, consciously or unconsciously, in relationships. So the best Bible application usually comes when we allow others to shine God's light on our lives and then use loving affirmation and sensitive pushing to help us grow.

The relationship between Paul and Onesimus that the letter to Philemon reveals is a good example of this kind of accountability. In love, they were able to accept each other. But also in love, they demanded the most from the other. This loving demand eventually led Onesimus, probably over his fears, to take a risk and face his past. Imagine what a strong man of God must have emerged from this experience! And then think what would have happened if he had been too proud to face Paul's loving demands and had struck out on his own in Rome. He would have missed important experiences of faith: reconciliation, forgiveness and the risk-taking side of Christian growth. Chances are he would have stayed a "baby Christian" for the rest of his life.

Every person is chicken in some way. Some are scared of emotions, others are fearful to face a traumatic incident in their past that still haunts them. Some are ruled by major sin issues because they are terrified that if they seek help to overcome their guilt, they will be rejected. Some are too frightened to take what to others are simple steps of faith, while others face monumental stresses alone because they don't want others to share their pain.

Whatever kind of person you are, finding a fellow disciple who is not afraid to admit to frailty can be a freeing experience. Instead of being lulled by a "nice little" Bible study, you can then be free to "get down and dirty" in God's Word! There's a big difference between the two approaches.

Which will you choose? If you choose growth, then God will honor you—not with an easy life but by producing depth of character that will grow with time and experience.

How does this step work? You simply take the questions you asked of yourself in the previous step and attempt to improve in as many areas as possible. Sometimes this will involve a conscious effort to change an attitude or thought pattern. Other times you will involve a friend to point out when you act destructively or make a negative comment. Throughout the process you will need to ask the Holy Spirit to balance your life with a healthy emphasis on God's grace along with the work you will do for your own growth. You don't want to get task-oriented or prideful. But you also want to avoid being a spiritual fatalist, taking no responsibility for your own life. As God speaks to you through his Spirit, you can find the balance and act appropriately.

Walk in the Light!

Jesus told Nicodemus to choose to walk in the Light. Your challenge in this chapter is the same. You have seen how Scripture can help you confront issues of personal growth and how important it is to find out how the Bible text applies to your life.

So walk in the light of God's Word, alongside at least one other growing disciple. As you consciously grow by applying God's Word, you will find that obedience produces joy, as Christ told his disciples:

If you obey my commands, you will remain in my love, just as I have obeyed my Father's commands and remain in his love. I have told you this so that my joy may be in you and that your joy may be complete. (Jn 15:10-11)

Personal Study and Reflection

1. Begin an application page in your study notebook. Write the following outline on this page:

Part 1: What was expected of them? (Here you'll develop a clear, comprehensive application for the original hearers or readers of the text you're studying.)

Part 2: How do I fit in? (You will identify ways in which you are like the recipients or characters of the text.)

1.

2.

3. etc.

Part 3: What is expected of me? (Prayerfully write down several things you can do to apply this Scripture.)

2. Turn to Malachi 2:17—3:5 and fill out the outline to the best of your ability. Work prayerfully.

Digging Deeper in Group Study

1. Discuss: In what ways did each of you identify with the recipients or characters of Malachi 2:17—3:5 (part 2 above)?

2. Discuss: How do you intend to apply what you learned from this Scripture?

3. Interactive exercise: Find some newspapers or magazines and cut out advertisements from them. For each, develop a "statement of response" (in other words, what does the advertiser want the reader to do?).

How is the response called for in the ads similar to the way response is called for in the Bible? How is it different?

8

MOVING
BEYOND
APPLICATION

For God, who said, "Let light shine out of darkness," made his light shine in our hearts to give us the light of the knowledge of the glory of God in the face of Christ. But we have this treasure in jars of clay to show that this all-surpassing power is from God and not from us. (2 Cor 4:6-7)

In my early teen years I knew a woman named India Majors. I never knew her extremely well, nor did I know much about her past. What I did know was that she possessed a deep, warm beauty that was attractive to me.

She was sick when we first met, and she remained sick during the few years I was privileged to know her. She was dying, and she knew it. You might say that most of the pages of her book had been written, and her final chapter in this life was drawing to a close.

But she was prepared to pass on. I have probably never met another person like her, but I know that I want to find the qualities that she exhibited, indeed was. For although she had spent her life in humble domestic service, her demeanor was somehow so beautiful that I longed to be like her. She lived in a tiny three-room cottage on the grounds of the people she had served for years, and she subsisted on Social Security, but she had a wealth of joy and life experience. Although she was in pain, she showed interest in me and helped me grow.

And she knew the Savior. Her faith ran like a stream through every part of her being. When I visited we didn't have much to say, since I was an active teen and she an older woman. And I can't say that I saw her regularly. But sometimes I would get an urge to visit her, and when I did I was blessed.

Even writing about her makes my heart full, as if she were still alive, still able to influence me. I know this to be true. Like the old leather volumes that my father has always collected and treasured, both for their content and for the beauty of their binding, this woman's pages were full of blessed life, wrapped gently in a soft, well-used binding. When I think of Mrs. Majors I can understand Paul's words in 2 Corinthians: "We have this treasure in jars of clay."

Searching for the Secret

I write of Mrs. Majors in this chapter because she had somehow captured the essence of life—peace. If her whole life was an equation, then the sum of all the parts equaled that elusive fruit of the Spirit that many want but few possess.

Our lives reflect our own quests for peace. We try out different combinations during the course of our lives—relationships, power, work, education, money, drugs, religion. What many find, however, is that no matter what they do there is no peace. Nothing can take the "noise" of life away, although the search intensifies as life progresses.

We tend to think of alcoholism, drug abuse, sexual addiction and violence as shortcuts people try to take in their search for peace. But there are other ways as well. Workaholics are people who get their greatest pleasure from work, and they are willing to sacrifice relationships and health on the altar of accomplishment. At the other extreme are people who are not able to accomplish even the simplest tasks because they have learned to feel "secure" with low esteem. Other "respectable" or socially acceptable addictions are sports, gossip, church (yes, even church!), guilt, money, food and pleasure. Relational addictions can include low self-esteem, complaining, hunger for power and self-pity.

Many mental-health experts believe that every person in our culture has some form of addiction. An addiction is anything that has been given an unhealthy priority in one's life for the purpose of meeting core inner needs. What is yours?

Addictions are a cheap imitation of the real thing; we use them to try to fill up our longing for God. That means an addiction is idolatry, a violation of the first two of the Ten Commandments.

Two Streams Come Together

One problem, two solutions. As we seek peace, will we choose God's way or our ways? Most of us unwittingly choose our own, and they don't work. It's God's way that leads to true peace, and Mrs. Majors found it.

So we need to ask some inductive questions: How did Mrs. India Majors capture peace when most cannot find it? Was it her personality, or did she do something right? And if she did know an important secret, how did a simple domestic worker figure it out?

Our search for answers of necessity leads to application. To state it very simply, because we believe God's promises in the Bible, if we learn and live God's way, we will experience peace. And when we learn and live, we are doing application.

It's helpful to think of the application process as involving two streams that run together. One is God's Word and our reading and interpretation of its truths. The other is our own life with its unique circumstances, choices and problems. In the last chapter we dealt with the first stream: understanding Scripture and discovering what it says to us.

Now in this chapter we turn the inductive process on our lives, asking the same kinds of questions that we asked of Scripture passages. We ask ourselves these questions because we want to discern God's plan for us as we pursue peace.

In the Garden

To discover God's plan for your life and mine we would do well to turn to Genesis and Revelation, the first and last chapters in our book of Scriptures. Remember how I liked to begin a Western novel by reading the first page or two and then skipping to the end? I believe that approach is helpful in approaching the Bible as well.

As you read the first chapters of Genesis and the last chapters of Revelation, you may well notice that they have a similar story, but the stories are inverse. In Genesis, God created an idyllic world that was marred by sin. Revelation shows how a sinful world will find redemption and perfection by the action of God.

We should ask ourselves what the interim must be like. We know what it's like to live in a chaotic creation, but is that God's plan for the time between the Fall and heaven—that we live in turmoil? If we read the Bible well, we find that the answer is no. I believe from reading the pages between "Paradise Lost" and "Paradise Restored" that we are directed to seek Eden's, and heaven's, lifestyle.

In the church we often speak of the results of sin, but perhaps we could change our focus a little by asking a question such as this: "How can we, by God's grace, move closer to Eden's (and heaven's) depiction of live in God's will?" Notice that this question assumes Christians are required to seek Eden's happiness and joy in life. That is precisely what the Christian life is all about: a committed, persistent desire to grow in grace and obedience so that we experience true joy. This kind of life is what we pray for in the Lord's Prayer: "Your kingdom [Garden of Eden? heaven?] come, your will be done, on earth as it is in heaven."

If we go back to Genesis, we can pick out three separate activities of God and the first human beings—activities carried out in a perfect balance in a perfect world. They are *relationship, rule* and *recreation.* Or, put another way, community building, meaningful work and leisure time. We see relationship within the Godhead ("let us make man," 1:26), between God and human beings, and between the first man and woman. There is work: God created the world, then put man and woman to work in his garden. And there is recreation, for God stopped and enjoyed his creation.

In this chapter we will examine each of these three aspects of a healthy, balanced life.

Building Healthy Relationships

The word *relationship* encompasses all of the Bible message. Obedience and disobedience are issues in relationship. Faith, hope and love are factors of relationship, as are knowledge and truth. When we work, it is to be for the good of others and to the glory of God. When we play, we enjoy our own bodies and minds in tandem with others. Everything we do in life is relational. Healthy relationships lead to peace; unhealthy ones lead to discord. Healthy relationships point to maturity, unhealthy ones to immaturity.

It is easy to forget the relational aspect of life. Church dogmas are easier put on paper than they are applied in relationship. It is less threatening to discuss a theological tenet or an aspect of church history than to delve into how people relate to one another in family, why we gossip about one another or how to apply true honesty in relationships.

It is precisely at the point of relational growth that Christians often get short-circuited. We speak of being "spiritual" while allowing families to fall apart. We talk about love while we lavish the latest toys upon our children—toys that can never fill their inner void. We get sidetracked by building programs, personal pews and whether there are to be flowers on the altar. We worry about bulletins, parking lots, office machinery and locks on buildings, as if beautifying our church made us better Christians. Worse, we allow the evil one to divide and conquer by playing off the normal tension that comes in relationships. As a result, churches are known for bickering, bitterness, division and gossip. That is exactly what Satan accomplished in Eden when he damaged the divine-human relationship, then turned Adam and Eve on each other.

If you take a good hard look at your own life, you may see how inconsistent you have become in relation to the created order. As a Christian you are called to grow continually in relation to God, self and others ("Love the Lord your God with all your heart and with all your soul and with all your mind and with all your strength"; "love your neighbor as yourself"). How much time do you spend building relationships? Do you spend quantity as well as quality time with your closest relatives and friends (especially your children and spouse)? What are your strongest relationships, and why? Which are your weakest ones?

Christian growth and maturity manifests itself in healthy relationships. Are you ready to take the next steps in your faith? You would do well to answer the following question each day: Does each of my relationships reflect my growth in maturity, so that I am becoming more like Jesus Christ in the way I interact with God, spouse, children, close friends, neighbors, associates, people I dislike, others?

Meaningful Work
Think about this scenario from a typical day: At 6:30 a.m. the alarm sounds. You climb out of the bed and turn on the radio to get news and weather. There are showers to be taken, children to be dressed, cups of coffee to

be downed; then it's off to work. On the way to work, you absent-mindedly listen to music while you fight the morning traffic.

At work a host of yesterday's problems confront you, and you immediately apply yourself to meeting their challenges. Phone calls, meetings, errands and obligations leave you little time to relax. Then you again confront a radio, a car and the traffic at the end of the workday.

The end of the workday does not signal the end of your day. There are chores, newspapers, meals and television shows. Finally the day ends, and with a murmured prayer you climb into bed. The next day everything starts over, with no time to relax in between.

Many people in our society live in three separate worlds. There is work, lived either at a frenetic pace or in dreary clock-watching. There is the home life, often including much mindless television viewing. And there is "Miller time," the leisure hours in which we attempt to "get away from it all."

Unfortunately, there are two glaring difficulties with such a lifestyle. First, our time spent in each is not lived for a higher purpose. Work time should be spent to the glory of God, reflecting integrity, Christian character and healthy relational witness. Time at home should reflect the value placed on relationship building. And recreation should include time for reflection, processing life, setting priorities, play and the enjoyment of God.

Second, we don't balance our lives well. Some people work far too much, others spend too much time in unhealthy recreation. In many families one spouse works constantly while the other does not seem able to find wholeness in a life's calling, whatever that may be.

In Eden (and we can presume in heaven as well) work was a God-honoring exercise, full of joy. Do you find this kind of satisfaction in your work today? Or does it consume you, or leave you dry? What does God want from your work, and how can you begin to fulfill your life's calling in a healthy way?

Energizing Recreation

Next to healthy relationship building, perhaps the most neglected aspect of personal life is time spent in introspection or recreation. Genesis tells us that after God created the world he "rested." He took time to enjoy, to reflect, to savor.

Healthy introspection allows us to slow down and gain perspective. Life has a tendency to come flying by in bits and bites, just as contemporary commercials toss out a dazzling series of unrelated images. Unless we slow down, we're doomed to getting caught in a flow that is unhealthy. As many people reach middle age they come to the sad realization that they are disillusioned, that their lives have been wasted chasing the wrong things. Introspection provides an escape from the trap of busyness—a way to gain perspective and decide on a new direction if that is needed.

The key character attribute necessary to healthy introspection is humility. Humility is the willingness to realize one's mistakes, to reach beyond oneself for answers, to accept nothing less for oneself than consistent and persistent growth. Humility allows us to look at ourselves with honest eyes, and it is a rare and beautiful quality.

Humble introspection can be carried out in several ways. First, there is *reflection*. When we reflect, we "replay" parts of our life and, with prayerful consideration, can be shown areas that need work. Reflection is effectively carried out in prayer and journaling. At least two or three times per week I sit down at my computer and spend quality time in reflection. I write about current tensions, the way I feel, how I am acting and reacting. Through this process I try to understand myself, my actions, thoughts, words. I do this because I want to grow.

Then I write a prayer based on the journal. This accomplishes a number of things, the most important being that I ask God to be the Lord of my feelings, actions, moods and desires. And it means that I go through all experiences in tandem with God. The result is that I'm better able to understand and deal with difficult circumstances.

Introspection also takes the form of *meditation*. The ancient Jewish/ Christian art of meditation involves careful, leisurely examination and application of God's Word. Imagine memorizing a verse, then slowly mulling over that verse as you wash dishes, drive your car, mow your lawn. Allow it to permeate your deepest thought patterns. Eventually, that verse will become part of who you are and how you think. This is what is accomplished through meditation.

Psalm 1 speaks of a person who "meditates day and night" on God's law. "He is like a tree planted by streams of water, which yields its fruit in season and whose leaf does not wither." You cannot reflect for long on a portion of Scripture without turning the light of God's Word upon your soul and allowing it to illumine your being.

And finally, there is *praise and thanksgiving*. Worshiping God keeps in focus the fact that an all-powerful God is in control of his creation. When we offer thanks to God, we count what we have been given and are diverted from the continuous search for more. When we praise him, we release our hearts to our heart's desire, and so we keep ourselves pure for him.

The Sum Total

How do you feel about yourself after reading the previous sections? Do you work each day as if called by God, at the same time loving those around you? Do you have a strong family, and do you put time and energy into building healthy relationships? Do you take quality leisure time to think, reflect, meditate, praise and give thanks?

And can you see how these activities bring peace? Living God's way over a lifetime will lead you to great joy. But how can you bring yourself from where you are to where God wants you to be?

Begin today to take the small steps necessary to growth. Take out a pad of paper and begin a journal. Write down what you know about yourself, your shortcomings, your failings, your gifts, your strong points. Get to know yourself, your behavior, your past. And as you meet yourself on a deeper level, prepare to move forward into the future. Consistent study of Scripture through the inductive process will allow you to meet God on a deeper level as well.

This week's personal reflection assignment will give you an opportunity to practice what this chapter preaches. Use your opportunity well.

Mrs. Majors, my elderly friend, lived a balanced life. She took plenty of time to develop her relationship with God and was reflective. She had many friends who had benefited from her love.

And she was at peace. What about you?

Personal Study and Reflection

1. Continue in your inductive study notebook, or begin a new one. Write the date at the top of the first page, and then you might consider putting the following outline on the paper (your own words and order are best).

Reflection:

Journal (record of events and your actions, feelings, attitudes)

Prayer (written prayers to God flowing from your journal)

Worship:

Enjoying God (words of appreciation for the Lord as you think about and interact with him)

Meditation:

Listening (your impressions as you quietly listen to God's Word)

2. At least two times during this week, fill out each section, using Malachi 2:17—3:5 to guide your thoughts (especially in meditation).

Digging Deeper in Group Study

1. Discuss: How did everyone do with the assignments for this week?

2. Discuss: What was one thing that people learned about themselves, and how do they feel about what they learned?

3. Discuss: What was one thing that people appreciated about God as they meditated and praised him?

4. Interactive exercise: Spend some time in Malachi 2:17— 3:5, meditating and worshiping. As you do, you may follow these steps:

a. Read through the passage slowly, verse by verse, allowing people to share what strikes them as the Scripture is read. Expand on images (like "purifier of silver"), talk about things learned in prior weeks. As a group, meditate on the passage.

b. Now read through the passage again, this time noting everything that can be learned about God—his character, actions and love. Write these down if you wish.

c. Spend some time in prayer, praising and thanking God for what was learned in part b.

USING INDUCTIVE METHODS IN GROUP AND INDIVIDUAL STUDY

Y ou prepare for your small group meeting each week by working twelve hours on one passage of Scripture. Before the meeting you run home, grab a quick bite of food, back the truck into the garage and bring out ten boxes of documented notes that you were able to garner from this week's study. Arriving at the home where your group will meet, you unpack your boxes, take your place and begin sifting through mounds of paper. As the Bible study starts, you and others in the group begin to work through the papers until finally all surfaces in the room are covered with paper, you and the others have disappeared in its mass, and the study has to end for the evening. You will return next week to continue your five-year study in the book of Ephesians . . .

Sound like fun? You can imagine that a slightly less drastic version of this scenario could play out in reality if everyone in a group prepared a step-by-step inductive study of a passage every week.

I'm not trying to set you up for that sort of experience. My purpose is to give you a "case of tools" that you can use when reading the Bible. While you may have had to prepare in detail for group work while working through this book, you won't always walk around with thick notebooks, thinking intently about small portions of Scripture for weeks on end (although you can certainly gain great benefits from doing just that!).

But you _will_ want to keep using inductive study, since it is the lay person's best tool for accurately reading and applying Scripture. So this chapter is dedicated to helping groups and individuals discover how they can use inductive study in a reasonable way. We will ask and answer questions related to shortening the inductive process, maintaining quality of study, knowing what to study and discerning where to turn for help.

Streamlining the Process
Is there a way to delve into a book of the Bible without doing extensive overview work?

Yes. The last thing anyone needs is to get bogged down _preparing_ to study a Bible book.

A good step would be to buy a study Bible (see appendix three for resource suggestions), complete with an introduction and an outline preceding each book of the Bible. A thorough reading of the introduction, plus one complete read-through of the book, will serve as excellent preparation for deeper study within the book itself.

If a group is planning to do a study, have each person read an introduction to the book and read through the book once; then use your first group session to share what you have learned through this overview. Discuss "who," "where" and "when" together; this will guide the study of individual passages.

Then you can break the book into meaningful units of study over an agreed-upon number of weeks (six to twelve) and move inductively through the book.

Is there a way to shorten the inductive study process so that an individual or group can move through a Bible book in a shorter time with less work?

Yes, with several possibilities. One way is to break down each book you are studying so that you don't necessarily study each passage on your way through. Instead, you study what you consider to be the most important passages in a book. This is a highly selective way of doing inductive study, but it still allows you to glean a book's most important message.

Another way to streamline is to consider the process itself. If you did a good overview of the book, your answers to "who," "where" and "when" will cut down on the time you must spend in a particular passage. You can shorten the interpretation stage by cutting our outlining and structural analysis. And if you are doing inductive study in a group, you can cut the personal application stage by leaving it for group time.

A final way to shorten the work requirement is to buy an inductive study guide that will lead you through a particular book of the Bible. The list of resources in appendix three can guide your choice.

Maintaining Quality

If we try to save time in inductive study, won't we sacrifice quality?

Not necessarily. There are ways to ensure continued quality. First, once a whole group has gone through this course you will have all learned how to read the Bible, and if you use these skills consistently they won't leave you. You can balance each other in knowledge and accountability. Second, one way you can save time in inductive study is to buy guides geared to inductive study; most of those currently on the market are of excellent quality. Third, the purpose of inductive study is to help you arrive at a purpose statement and personal application. If you are able to reach these goals with an abbreviated form of inductive study, then you are doing effective and accurate study of the Bible.

There is another way you can benefit from inductive study without the intense, detailed work required in this course. You can carefully lay out a particular book of the Bible, then divide the various passages of the book among group members. Each individual can then do a detailed study of his or her particular passage, passing out questions in advance so that everyone comes to the group study prepared. Your use of people's time will be efficient, quality will be high, and you can learn from one another.

What will keep inductive study from degenerating into an academic exercise?

Much prayer. One of the greatest, and most valid, criticisms of Bible study groups is that over time they become academic and ingrown rather than mission-oriented. Yet this is not the fault of Bible study per se. Bible study should lead one to become God's person in the world. From cover to cover the Bible challenges us to be servants, to share God's love with a world in need. The Bible itself challenges the ingrown Bible study group.

So it is groups or individuals who bear the responsibility when they have become sidetracked from Christian growth. When a group becomes ingrown or academic, it is not approaching the Bible in the appropriate way.

If you are looking for the right "recipe," begin with God's Word, add plenty of humility, and sprinkle in self-examination, integrity and attention to detail. And beat this mixture with love.

Keep studying the Bible, but add the above ingredients, and you will avoid the "academic" label. Instead you may well be called "sons and daughters of the Most High."

When we get together we want to do more than go through passages using inductive study.

Great! If people are doing their work at home, then you don't need to spend lots of group time rehashing what you learned. Instead, you are free to concentrate on discussing and applying God's truth. More on this in the next chapter.

Knowing What to Study

Won't we eventually run out of books of the Bible to study inductively?

How? There are sixty-six books of the Bible that you can study. Not all lend themselves easily to inductive study, but all are a part of God's Word. Assuming you could get through all or most of the books in a lifetime using inductive study, wouldn't it make sense to begin again, since you can never mine the depths and riches of God's Word?

But this question raises a valid point. That is, *what* should your group study? How can a group pick a book of the Bible that is most appropriate for its situation?

Before answering that question, let's sweep through the Bible, surveying its history and themes briefly.

The Old Testament. Many Christians are frustrated when they try to read the Old Testament. It was written to an ancient people who lived many thousands of years ago, and the culture of that people is difficult to understand. Moreover, some see the God of the Old Testament as a God of judgment. Instead of grappling with the difficulties, much of the church chooses to stay in the New Testament.

It is sad when this happens. True, the Old Testament is sometimes difficult to understand. But it does constitute a rich treasury of wisdom and history, and the Bible would be incomplete without it. In the Old Testament we learn about the beginning of human history and even time itself. We can trace the history of God's dealings with men and women from the Garden of Eden to Mount Sinai, from Egypt to Israel. And if we listen closely enough, we can hear the longing, mournful cry of a sinful and oppressed people seeking their Messiah.

But how can today's Christian get through the long genealogies in Genesis and elsewhere, the strict, intricately detailed guidelines for worship in Leviticus, and the often repetitive prophecies contained in Isaiah and Jeremiah to interact with the Bible from a modern-day perspective? It is difficult, to be sure, but not impossible. And the one who is willing to pay the price is blessed.

People often encounter the Old Testament sometime after a New Year's resolution, when they are working through the Bible book by book. They get bogged down at the end of Exodus and downright discouraged in Leviticus, and then give up in frustration. This approach doesn't work because it starts from the wrong point. It is hard to enjoy a part of history if you haven't first been given the larger context. How will we understand the years just before the Civil War without first having an overall grasp of American history? In isolation, this period could be difficult to master and boring to study. But a study of the Civil War comes alive when undertaken within the context of two hundred years of American life. Race relations, the role of the federal government and interstate tensions have been issues throughout our history.

The Old Testament has its own "big story" to tell, one in which God's imprint is strong and firm. It records the story of a nation, Israel, and that nation's dealings with God and other nations. It is not merely a historical record; it is a series of chronicles recorded within a theological perspective.

There are three basic parts to the Old Testament: the Books of History (the first seventeen), the Books of Poetry (Job, Psalms, Proverbs, Ecclesiastes, Song of Songs) and the Books of Prophecy (from Isaiah to Malachi). The Books of History contain historical narrative as well as the detailed giving of the law of Moses at Mount Sinai. The Books of Poetry transcend the Old Testament time, although much of their writing is focused in the high point of Israel's history under King David and King Solomon. And the Books of Prophecy, alternating between words of judgment and words of promise, speak against sins the Israelites committed throughout their history.

Further analysis shows that the Books of History primarily deal with the history of Israel from the beginning of time through about 600 B.C., when Israel fell and was taken captive by other nations. The Books of Poetry were written mostly around 1000 B.C., and the Books of Prophecy were written generally from 900 to 400 B.C. This means that although the Old Testament is not a chronological work, as you read through it the time generally runs chronologically (there are exceptions, of course).

Although each book was written to address different circumstances, certain themes can be traced throughout the Old Testament. One well-recognized theme is that of covenant (or promise). Another favored by some Bible scholars is typology—New Testament realities are represented by "types" (symbols) in the Old Testament (an example is the Old Testament system of sacrifices, which was fulfilled in Jesus Christ). Still another is the aspect of redemption, the theme of "paradise lost" (and "paradise regained" in the New Testament).

The covenant theme. I believe that the idea of covenant is central to the story of the Old Testament (and of the New Testament as well). The Bible is a book about relationships, and covenants govern relationships. If you think about it, every relationship in life, whether it is related to work, family or even sports, has its covenantal understandings.

In the Old Testament, the original covenant between God and humanity was made in the Garden of Eden. The agreement was simple: If we stayed away from the tree of the knowledge of good and evil, we would live in God's garden forever. The purpose of the original agreement was just as simple: As long as we lived within God's will, we would know life and peace.

When we sinned that original covenant was marred; it was replaced by what is commonly known as the covenant of grace. Under this covenant, which is not really very different from the original covenant, God agrees to forgive our sins and live in relationship with us, and we agree to live under God's lordship. From our perspective, it's a wonderful bargain!

The Old Testament story shows, however, how we continually broke our covenant with God. The Books of History depict the sin, the Books of Poetry cry out because of sin, and the Books of Prophecy call out for repentance. Fortunately, the Old Testament story also depicts a God of grace and mercy who continually offers a restored relationship to those willing to accept his offer. We do not need to read the Old Testament to learn about the characters that inhabit its pages—we understand them all too well, for we are sinners like them. Instead, we read the Old Testament to fall in love with a God who passionately desires a deeper relationship with his people.

Studying the Old Testament. Many people would be surprised to hear that the Old Testament speaks of a God of mercy and grace. A commonly held misconception is that the Old Testament speaks solely of a God of judgment. This is not the case. There are strong statements and events that are difficult to understand, it's true. But God's covenant was given to a primitive, warlike people. A covenant given to people in ancient times would be very different in many circumstances from one given to people in our day (although it actually might be difficult to convince ancient people that we aren't more warlike and sadistic than they). The beauty of the Bible is that God was so eager to reach the Hebrews that he was willing to speak in the language they understood. The ancient Jewish people, surrounded by child-sacrificing pagans and all too willing to adopt such rituals themselves, needed a firm hand and strict guidelines.

So where do you begin your study? The answer depends on your needs. What do you need to learn? Do you continually slip in your relationship with God? Then Deuteronomy, a "second giving of the law" in which Moses essentially preaches a set of very long sermons, is for you. Do you struggle with the problem of evil? Job is well known, but Habakkuk is equally good. Want a strong word of judgment coupled with solid promises? Read Isaiah. Psalms is a book of prayers that were sung in the temple. Song of Songs is a book about passionate love, often thought to describe the church's relationship with God, but appropriate for a couple wanting deeper intimacy. Jonah is about a man who ran from his responsibility to God and others. Ezra and Nehemiah tell of the rebuilding of the temple and the city of Jerusalem after they had been destroyed. They would be good books for inner-city workers who live daily amid drugs, violence and families in distress. And what about Malachi? He spoke to a nation that had forgotten its God and neglected worship. We could all profit from listening to Malachi's word from the Lord.

A good Bible handbook, such as Halley's, would provide good overviews of the books of the Old Testament so that you can make an intelligent choice. If you take the time to look you'll find that the Old Testament offers many wonderful possibilities for study.

The New Testament. Though the New Testament is shorter than the Old, it too can be divided into distinct sections. First there are the historical books, which include the Gospels (*gospel* means "good news"). Matthew, Mark, Luke and John are Gospels. Acts is a historical book as well, telling the story of the early church's beginnings and the "acts of the Holy Spirit" that spurred its growth.

Then there are the letters, also called *epistles,* which make up the bulk of the New Testament. These are letters to individuals, churches and groups of churches, beginning with Romans and concluding with Jude. They address many of the problems of the early church and follow a fairly predictable form, which includes an introduction (identification of author and recipients), a salutation (greeting), a thanksgiving and prayer in which the author expresses joys and concerns about the recipients, the body of the letter, and the benediction (farewell). An interesting sidelight is that the body of the letter is often an elaboration of concerns raised in the prayer. So when you are studying a letter it makes sense to go to the prayer in a letter (although some do not have one) to find out what the rest of the book is about.

The final category of writing in the New Testament is called apocalyptic literature, and only one falls into this category: the Revelation of St. John. Although it is a letter (a "circular letter," meaning that it was written to a group of churches), it is commonly called apocalyptic writing because it speaks in graphic detail about the end of time.

A new way of looking at the covenant. The New Testament picks up where the Old Testament ends, continuing the story of our relationship with God. With the coming of Jesus Christ, God broke all barriers in his desire to develop a relationship with his rebellious created ones. Jesus willingly subjected himself to his own creation, living as a common servant and dying as a common criminal. His resurrection from the dead was enough to break the bonds of sin and to free us to pursue a life of peace. When you and I claim to be Christians, we say that we have a living, vital relationship with Jesus Christ. Our part of the covenant involves asking Jesus Christ to be our Lord. In return, we are given restoration and the privileges of adoption into God's family—God's part of the covenant.

A fascinating change from Old Testament times to New involves the vehicle God uses to bring his blessing. In the Old Testament God called a people, one nation. His plan was to bless them so that they in turn could lead other nations into the active pursuit of God. In the New Testament God chose to spread his kingdom across racial barriers. The unifying plan of God is twofold: first, each Christian has salvation through Jesus Christ; second, every Christian has been brought into a "kingdom"—God's family, the church. The demise of the church in certain parts of the world today has not come because God didn't have a big enough plan. It's because we undersell and underlive this plan.

Studying the New Testament. You will undoubtedly find that choosing and studying a New Testament book is much easier than doing the same with an Old Testament book. That's because the New Testament was written to believers after the ascension of Jesus Christ—us! Each New Testament book was written either directly to the church or for the church's use.

With the exception of Revelation, which is difficult for group study (but not impossible!), most New Testament books are not difficult to study. This part of the Bible is a rich resource of challenging material.

Just remember: don't forget the Old Testament. It may take a little more work, but it is still God's Word.

What books would be helpful for a group or individual just beginning to do inductive Bible study?

In the Old Testament, any of the following: Ruth (history), Ecclesiastes (poetry), Jonah (combination of prophecy and history), Habakkuk (prophecy/poetry combination) or Micah (prophecy). In the New Testament, I would suggest Mark, any of the letters between Galatians and Colossians, or James, 1 Peter, 1 John or Jude.

Where can we turn for Bible helps, and which would you suggest?

I suggest that you get a good study Bible, a Bible dictionary and a concordance. Optional would be an almanac and Bible handbook.

For specific suggestions in each of these categories, and for help in picking study guides, turn to appendix three. There I have compiled a brief bibliography of helpful resources.

The Goal

As you make your decisions, remember that your study of God's Word is a means to an end: that you and your fellow students will grow daily as Christ's disciples. There is nothing more exciting than growing into oneness with God through his Word.

So choose carefully what you will study, and prayerfully consider what God would have you learn.

Personal Study and Reflection

Do an abbreviated inductive study of Malachi 3:6-12. Since some of the work has already been done, you may want to follow the following format.

Who

What

Why

Basic outline and analysis

Application for original readers

Digging Deeper in Group Study

1. Discuss: What did people learn from their inductive study of Malachi 3:6-12?

2. Discuss: Do application together. What does this passage mean to me? to our group? to our church?

3. Interactive exercise: To enhance what you have learned in this chapter, lay out a basic six-week inductive study of Malachi as if you were preparing to study it as a group. You will have to choose what you feel are the key passages that encompass the message of Malachi.

10

PREPARING AND LEADING AN INDUCTIVE BIBLE STUDY

You have been asked to lead your first inductive Bible study. With fear in your heart, you begin to prepare. Taking extensive notes on the passage before you, you dig deeply into the Word and learn as you work.

Eventually you sit back and take stock of the situation. You have taken pages and pages of notes, but you have no clue as to how you will communicate this mass of material to the people in your group. What now?

You begin to think inductively. Searching your memory, you ask: Who was a good teacher or leader in my past? How did she or he get through to the students? Why did I want to learn in that teacher's class?

Good Teachers Let Students Learn
When I ask myself these questions, my thoughts turn to two teachers I had

at seminary. They weren't necessarily "hotshot" teachers; as far as I knew there were no waiting lists for their classes. Yet they had a way of getting through to me—and, I suspect, to others—without appearing to "teach." In other words, they let the students learn.

Other teachers would use their allotted time to hand out myriad pages of information, yet several years into ministry I must say that I rarely use what they gave me. The reason? Since I am not a genius, there is no way I could retain all the information on counseling, theology, ancient languages, Christian education, and preaching that was thrown at me in seminary. In the ministry I need *tools* more than information.

The two teachers who helped me most gave me tools that I continue to use every day in life and ministry. Interestingly, both gave tools for Bible study. And they had very similar methods. Three statements can define their method:

☐ People learn more when they have to prepare.

☐ Teaching is more fulfilling when students are prepared.

☐ The best teachers make students prepare, then let the students lead.

I was expected to have something prepared each day the class met. Instead of expecting one major paper per semester, these teachers made us prepare to interact on every topic their courses covered. And because I was expected to participate in the discussion, I came mentally and emotionally prepared to talk about the subject.

Unfortunately, many students find this kind of class to be intimidating. In school we are taught to think of A's as the end result, not knowledge. Schools are not filled with hungry students but with people who expect information that has already been digested. There is much, much more to the learning process, but we don't always act like it.

I believe that this "feed-me-digested-food" expectation has carried over into the church. Perhaps you have felt insecure about doing "homework" as you worked through this book. There was the constant possibility of being "wrong." Homework has its risks. Yet there is a payoff for those who worked hard to prepare.

This chapter is not just dedicated to helping you learn what questions to ask as you lead inductive study, but to help you think about what makes the learning process meaningful. There are three things we'll consider in relation to preparing and leading an inductive Bible study. First, we will discuss ways to help fellow disciples prepare for the learning event. Second, we will examine principles that make the learning event more meaningful. And finally, we will talk about small group dynamics and how the group itself must be constructed. The goal of this chapter is that you begin to think about the learning event and how to make it effective—perhaps as a teacher, leader or facilitator, but definitely as a student.

Preparing for the Learning Event

If you want to do a thorough job of leading an inductive Bible study, you should prepare in advance so that you can give group members a set of questions at least a week before the study begins. Remember, the best teachers find a way to let the students prepare before the event.

So using all you have learned in this book and in practice, do a complete inductive study of your passage. In the end, as you know, you have a statement of author's intent and statement of application.

Then, develop a purpose statement for the learning event that will flow from your findings. The reason for doing this is very simple: a purpose statement will guide your questioning. Maintaining focus allows you to chart a positive direction as you prepare for the study.

For practice, let's turn again to Philemon 12-16. If you recall our work from previous chapters, we came up with the following statement of application:

> In response, Philemon should forgive and accept Onesimus as a brother in Christ, but—equally important—he must learn to see worth in people, minister to them in Christ's name and invest his life in them, nurturing them in Christ's love.

Now, how would you write a purpose statement for the learning event you are contemplating?

Here's what I would say: *The purpose of this study is to demonstrate the high cost of love that is required if we seek to impact people's lives for Christ.*

You are now ready to write the homework questions. And the approach to this task is very simple: Take the results of your study, the mass of notes, and ask questions that aim toward your purpose statement. Your questions can follow the three steps of inductive study—observation, interpretation and application.

One note before proceeding: It may be helpful to keep some of the deeper, more probing questions for the group study session so that the gathering of the group is not anticlimactic. If everyone came knowing everything about the passage being studied, there would be little need for a group time.

Observation. All you really need to do here is to take some of your observations and turn them into questions. We observed the following: the author wanted to keep the one being sent; the author was in chains for preaching the gospel; the author was trying to convince the recipient to receive his slave as a brother in Christ.

Now, how would you write questions from these observations?

Here are some possibilities:

☐ What is the author's relationship to the slave?

☐ What is the recipient's relationship to the slave?

☐ List everything that describes the slave. What kind of person had he been? What kind of person was he now?

Interpretation. Then come the deeper questions. What would you ask based on Philemon 12-16?

Here are a few possibilities:

☐ Why does Paul speak so forcefully about a slave?

☐ What rights did slaves have in Paul's day?

☐ How did Onesimus end up with Paul?

☐ Based on the tone of Paul's words, what concerned him about Philemon?

☐ What kind of transformation must Onesimus have gone through in order for him to return to his master a useful brother in Christ?

Application. Finally, you can begin to turn the study toward the student in preparation for the learning event:

☐ What did God require of Paul? of Onesimus? of Philemon?

☐ What positive characteristics do you find in Paul? in Onesimus?

And that's it! If you did good inductive study of a passage, then you are more than prepared; you are enough of an expert to write a helpful study.

The study homework questions don't have to be clever. They just need to get the students into God's Word so that your time together can be a positive time of exploring the meaning of the passage instead of a dry search for facts.

Making the Learning Event Meaningful

Imagine that you have prepared the group by providing a set of questions the week before the group is to meet. Further, the group members have opened the Scriptures and answered the questions.

Think how far ahead of most studies you already are! Now you don't need to take valuable group time to introduce each other to a passage of Scripture. Instead you can take seriously the words of Hebrews 10:24: "Let us consider how we may spur one another on toward love and good deeds."

The goal of Bible study. Before discussing how you should lead the actual Bible study session, let's back up for a moment and consider the goal of Bible study in general. Just what is it that we hope to accomplish when we open God's Word in community?

The way many study groups are operated, it would seem to be the extension of knowledge. Think of how many studies end up as theological battles, or in a search for small details that don't necessarily influence our lives. Some Bible studies never produce visible growth in their members. Still others, focusing on social interaction, don't delve deeply enough into God's Word to learn anything from it. These focus on "shared ignorance" rather than gleaning truth from God's Word.

Where is the happy medium between getting deep into God's Word and allowing people to "come as they are"? Is it possible to have an intense, in-depth Bible study that still changes people's lives? Of course, if you remember the goal. It is quite simple, stated in the Mosaic law and again by Jesus Christ himself: "Love the LORD your God with all your heart and with all your soul and with all your mind and with all your strength . . . and your neighbor as yourself" (Mk 12:30; see Deut 6:4-5 and Lev 19:18).

Put another way, the successful Bible study (or any church activity, for that matter) will contribute to relational growth. People who are learning from God's Word will begin to exhibit growth in their relationships to others. James says that the one who looks intently into God's Word and forgets what is there is like a man who looks in a mirror and walks away, immediately forgetting what he looks like (Jas 1:23-24)! It doesn't make sense to spend time listening to God's Word unless you plan to grow.

And what is the best way to grow? In community! Small groups offer the best, most intimate way for individuals and groups to grow within a church structure. As we have said before, a small group serious about God's Word is a mighty force.

The implications for actual Bible-study time are very important. First, remember that your primary reason for gathering is *people*, not *task*. If someone is hurting, then the group must attend to his need (which, by the way, teaches all in the group how to love their neighbor). If someone has a question, you must do all you can to answer her question. Small groups are families, and no good family would ignore a hurting member so that work could be finished. Remember, God's Word and prayer are communication. So is group time. Your group exists for communication that will lead into your being a community. Therefore you must listen to all in the group, from God down to the humblest member.

Second, if people are preparing the study beforehand, then God the Holy Spirit has had the opportunity to speak to them already, if they were willing to listen. The best opener for the Bible-study portion of a group session is to ask people what they are learning, what questions they have and how this passage has begun to shape their thinking. What a great Bible study is yours if the students come prepared to *teach* each other in this way!

Finally, instead of designing your group around study, design your study around group. Let God's Word contribute to community building and growth in love instead of imposing a structure that does not cause the group to grow. There are three things that will make the learning process contribute to community building.

Ask a "felt-need" opening question(s) that in a nonthreatening way identifies the individuals with the application in the passage of Scripture. In the time set aside by your group for community building, open with one or two questions that somehow relate to the passage being studied. This will do several things. First, every person will have the opportunity to share. Second, you are encouraging people to share about themselves, opening the way for deeper accountability and sharing within the context of God's Word. And third, you are emphasizing community as you enter the study portion of your time together.

What kinds of questions are helpful? Good "past, present and future" questions always work. A "past" question could be related to childhood: "What kinds of family rituals did your family observe for Christmas?" A "present" question could be this: "If you could give up one thing from your schedule each week, what would it be and why?" A "future" question would be, "One thing I would like to do in the coming year is . . ."

Then, as you draw attention to Scripture, let the discussion flow with the lives of the individuals in the group. Notice that I did not say to keep the discussion on the track you would like (based on your Purpose Statement). If they did the preparatory Bible study, then they know at least a part of where you want to go. A very short statement on your part would direct their attention to the application, but even this is not always necessary.

Notice as well that I did not say to let the discussion flow in *any* direction. Letting a discussion move helter-skelter with no discipline will sidetrack both Bible study and its application to your lives. There are hundreds of ways a discussion can get off-track, and when it's off-track you have made a mistake.

The best way to open the Bible study portion of the evening is to bring out the Bible, read the passage together, and ask people what they learned or what questions they had. A well-prepared group of students will be prepared to take it from there, with your gentle but firm guidance.

At some point you can bring out your "heavy hitters"—the questions you kept aside for the group meeting. In Philemon's case, you could focus attention on Paul: What is it about Paul's message that is so revolutionary? What is it about Paul's relationship with Onesimus that is so revolutionary? How are you like, or unlike, Paul in what he says and does in this passage?

It is always helpful to turn attention to the Scripture and to interact with the characters. Interacting with the characters of Scripture, whether they are protagonists of a story or recipients of a letter, allows you to bring a relational flair to the study and contributes to growth in love. Small groups should, above all, help us to understand and learn from ourselves and others. The Bible is a book about relationships. So good small groups will use the Bible to learn relationally.

Finally, close with a relevant statement of application. If the Bible study has been on track, many lessons will have been learned and application will have been made. But it is always helpful to close by pulling everything together and clearly showing where the study has led. This could, if done well, be accomplished in a few short reflective sentences leading into a prayer time.

Every group time needs a positive closing experience. You will do well to prepare your summary beforehand as a means of pointing back to the members' at-home preparation. Then you can adapt your plan in accordance with the insights that the Holy Spirit seems to be impressing on the group.

In the case of Philemon, you would want to draw attention to the idea of costly love, of investing in the lives of others as a manifestation of Christ's work in your own life.

Group Dynamics

There is a simple equation I developed for use in marriage counseling. I have since found it relevant in every aspect of relationship building, so here it is:

$$\text{Commitment} + \text{Communication} = \text{Community}$$

You may have everything that a good small group could want: a great church, positive leadership, deep Bible study, people who want to be in the group. But without community, you are only a noise on the landscape of church events (paraphrase of 1 Cor 13:1).

The small group must do all it can to facilitate the deepening of relationships and its group identity and unity. My book, *The Big Book on Small Groups* (Downers Grove, Ill.: InterVarsity Press, 1992), deals in-depth with small group issues and community building. Although we cannot go into much detail at this point, let's look at a few important issues related to commitment and communication so that you can focus on community building as you lead a Bible study.

Commitment. A healthy group will make several commitments—nonnegotiables that are essential for success. The first is *time.* Without a time set aside to meet on a consistent basis, the group will be hampered. Related to time is the commitment each member makes to being an integral part of the group, present each time the group meets.

The group must also commit itself to *shared growth.* What is it that will bring the group closer together if not the knowledge that "we are all in this together"? Small groups that thrive are successful for precisely this reason; conversely, if even one member lacks a desire to grow, the group will struggle.

Related to shared growth are *honesty and confidentiality*. People who are going deep into each other's lives need the security of knowing that everything that is shared will stay within the context of the group itself. If more Christians held to confidentiality, church groups would experience more honest conflict resolution and there would be less gossip.

There are other commitments the group must make in order to ensure a secure environment: agreements as to what happens during group time, what material will be studied and how long the group will be meeting together. These matters are best handled by a "group covenant," an agreement made between members of a group for a specific period of time (usually six weeks to six months). You can learn more about making covenants in some of the books on small groups that are on the market, including my own book referred to above.

Communication. If you think of commitment as the skeletal structure of the group's building, communication is the immediate environment in which the group meets. Communication is where the rubber meets the road in small groups. Included in healthy communication are honesty and confidentiality, listed above as commitments. Other components of good communication are healthy realism and a willingness to share, to laugh, to spend time together and to love each other.

The comfort of the meeting place is a major factor in communication. People need to physically feel at home before they will relax and have fun together. Put people in a cell, or even an office conference room, and it will take longer to break down relational walls than if you put the same group into a comfortable, well-lit, quiet, cozy living room. It makes a big difference.

And keep the noise down. Nothing is more distracting to a group than a phone that rings (and is answered by the host). Disconnect the phone, or turn down the ringer and use an answering machine. Children and pets can be distractions too. Perhaps pets could be put outside, while children are left with a sitter or directed to another room, or even kept with adults to join in the learning process.

The leader must be willing to lead. Groups by committee seldom work effectively. In my book on small groups I say that the foundation for effective small group ministry is well-trained leadership. Again, *The Big Book on Small Groups* offers guidelines that can help you learn to be a good leader.

One final aspect of preparation and group life needs to be emphasized: prayer. It is impossible to stay on top of the many dynamics and individual lives as you seek to grow in community—only God can do that. And only God can change a heart. When you pray, you show a willingness to let God work. And according to James 5:16, "the prayer of a righteous man is powerful and effective"!

Going from Here

With the Word of God in your hand and the tools of inductive study in your pocket, you are now ready to go forth as a worker for the kingdom of God. Use the tools—they are your friends. Share the gospel—it is your message. Build community—it is your goal. And by all means, allow yourself to be set free in God so that you can be the thinking, serving, growing Christian you were called to be.

Personal Study and Reflection

Take out the material from Malachi 3:6-12 that you worked on last week. Then begin a new page in your notebook and write in the following outline, leaving spaces between the items.

Write a one-sentence Purpose Statement for the learning event.

Write three or four questions under each of the following categories to guide a student's study:

☐ Observation
☐ Interpretation
☐ Application

Write three or four "heavy-hitter" questions that you will hold to ask during the group session.

Now fill in the outline, preparing a study based on Malachi 3:6-12.

Digging Deeper in Group Study

1. Discuss: What were some of the purpose statements for Malachi 3:6-12?
2. Interactive exercise: As a group, prepare for a learning event based on Malachi 3:6-12.

    a. Brainstorm three or four "past, present or future" questions that would, in a nonthreatening way, get students to talk about themselves, making sure that the questions somehow tie into the text being studied.

    b. Develop a set of "heavy-hitter" questions that you would like to see a group focus on when studying Malachi 3:6-12.

    c. Finally, discuss what application you would like to see a group come to, and then develop an activity that would cement what has been learned (for example, a reflective prayer time, a game, a brainstorming session, a role play).

APPENDIX 1:
USING THIS **B**OOK IN
GROUP OR
CLASSROOM **S**ETTINGS

There are a number of ways you can use this book as a training course. It can be read as a book and discussed. It can be part of a one-hour Sunday-school class. Or it can be used as part of a small group meeting that lasts one and a half to two hours. Regardless of the setting, I suggest that you use the course in its entirety, since every activity and homework assignment reinforces principles and ideas spoken of in the chapters. In addition, the "Digging Deeper in Group Study" material builds on the "Personal Study and Reflection" work.

A few ideas to keep in mind when using this book in a group or a classroom:

1. It is intentionally written as an empowering tool. This means that the shared approach to learning will be much more effective than a lecture approach. Allow the group to offer ideas and interact each week. The

"Digging Deeper in Group Study" section has been written for interaction, not for presentation within a lecture.

2. Group time should be spent working through the "Digging Deeper" material, since it is written with groups in mind. This material can be adapted and changed to fit different situations.

3. It is helpful to have in place a group covenant (agreement) that specifically covers such items as when to meet, how long (in weeks), what happens during meeting time, ground rules for communication and homework commitments. This covenant will allow the group to have a single identity and purpose so that fellow disciples can focus on learning and growing.

4. Allow a sharing time each week so that people can talk about their insecurities and frustrations. Not all people reading this book and undertaking the assigned work will understand every part. Letting group members be, and feel, human will go a long way toward helping them relax as they prepare each week for the learning event.

5. If possible, get the same Bible version for each student so that they can compare "apples and apples." I would suggest the New International Version, New King James Version, or New Revised Standard Version. Avoid using an amplified version like the Living Bible, since paraphrases don't lend themselves to inductive study.

6. Make sure that the place of meeting is comfortable, allows for eye contact (preferably in a circle of some sort), and free from distractions like phones and playing children.

7. A possible schedule:

    5-10 minutes for chatting and group building

    45-50 minutes for "Digging Deeper in Group Study" activities

    15 minutes for sharing and prayer

    15 minutes for refreshments

This one-and-a-half-hour schedule can be adapted for shorter or longer meetings as necessary.

APPENDIX 2: **C**HECKING **Y**OUR **W**ORK

*T*his section has been prepared as a means of checking the inductive work you are doing as you make your way through the chapters. I have done examples of the homework and group work so that you can check against a standard. Remember, don't look until after you have completed your work!

Chapter 1: Introducing the Inductive Process

Personal Study and Reflection

2. Inductive study is an interactive method of learning—a process of gathering, interpreting and applying information.

3. *Observation* is asking questions in order to "take apart" the components of what you are studying. *Interpretation* involves interacting with the infor-

mation gained through observation—putting the parts back together so that you begin to form a picture of the whole. And through *application* you attempt to discover how this newly gained understanding is relevant to your own life.

Chapter 2: Approaching the Study of a Bible Book

Personal Study and Reflection

1. Examples of "who" in Malachi

1:1: God speaks, he speaks to Israel, he speaks through Malachi.

1:3: God speaks of two brothers, Jacob and Esau, one he loved and the other he hated. God's tone is harsh, angry.

1:4: God is called Lord Almighty. He promises to crush Edom. Edom was planning to rebuild ruins, resulting from their being crushed.

1:5: The Lord Almighty is angry because he feels the priests have treated his name with contempt.

1:6—2:9: God speaks against priests.

2:11: God speaks against Judah, including Israel and Jerusalem.

2. Examples of "when"

1:4: Future promise given that if Edom rebuilds God will destroy.

2:4: God harks back to the covenant he made with Levi, the father of priests. This promise was still to stand, but was broken.

3:2: God will come as a judge.

3:17: There will be a day in which God comes to take up those who are obedient.

Chapter 4 speaks of coming judgment.

Note: The whole book speaks of events in the life of Judah that point to apathy and blatant sin.

3. Examples of "where"

1:3: Esau's place is a wasteland.

1:4: Edom.

1:7: The altar and the table of the Lord have been treated contemptuously.

1:10: God is angry about what happens in the temple.

1:11: God's name will be great among all nations.

2:11: Sin has been committed in Jerusalem and Israel.

3:1: God will come to his temple.

4. Examples of "what"

1:1-5: God will prove his love to Israel by his actions. God is angry because his love was even in question.

1:6-14: Priests were bringing contempt to the Lord's altar and table by their attitude and by accepting blemished sacrifices. God calls himself Lord Almighty several times. God says that his name is great, and that honor is due him.

2:19: God is angry at the priests, and threatens to curse them

a. for not honoring him with their hearts,

b. because they did not revere God,

c. and because they did not teach God's way and caused many to stumble.

Digging Deeper in Group Study

To summarize who, when, where and what:

Who: The prophet Malachi (Malachi means "my messenger"), acting as God's spokesman, brings a strong word from God against an apathetic, faithless Jewish people and their religious leadership.

When: Malachi wrote following the return from exile, after the temple and Jerusalem had been rebuilt and the people of Israel had time to settle in and forget their God.

Where: The focal point of this book was Jerusalem, especially the temple and its altar.

What: God, speaking through Malachi, addressed Israel's dead worship, cynical leadership, lack of purity, apathy and unwillingness to give.

Chapter 3: Discovering the Purpose and Structure of a Bible Book

Personal Study and Reflection

Summaries of who, when, where and what are above.

Author's intent (why): The purpose of Malachi was to warn the hypocritical Israelites and religious leaders that God the Almighty was still in control, that he wanted their hearts and their devotion, and that he was going to return as a judge.

Digging Deeper in Group Study

Key phrase in Malachi: God Almighty

  Outline

I. God Almighty's love for and active involvement with Israel is confirmed (1:1-5)

    A. "I have loved Israel" (1:1-3)

    B. "I am in control of events" (1:4-5)

II. The priests sinned against God Almighty (1:6—2:9)

    A. The priests abused their sacrificial duties (1:6-14)

    B. The priests did not honor the truth of God, nor did they teach it (2:1-9)

III. The people were unfaithful to God Almighty by intermarrying and divorcing (2:10-16)

IV. God Almighty will come to judge, punish and redeem his people (2:17—4:6)

    A. The Israelites questioned God's justice, but he will judge (2:17—3:5)

    B. The Israelites withheld their tithe, so God will withhold blessing (3:6-12)

    C. The Israelites thought it futile to serve God, but God rewards the righteous (3:13-18)

    D. God will come as judge against the wicked and will free the righteous (4:1-6)

Chapter 4: Learning to Observe

Personal Study and Reflection

Look (observations on Malachi 2:17—3:5)

2:17: The people have spoken; God is weary with their words; the people are cynical, believing that God rewards evil; the people want to know where the "God of justice" is.

3:1: God speaks; he will send a messenger to "prepare his way"; he will come suddenly; the people are "seeking" the Lord; the Lord will appear in his own temple; a "covenant" will be delivered by a messenger; the messenger is desired by the people; God is the Lord Almighty.

3:2: Author picks up speaking where God leaves off; author asks two questions: who can endure and who can stand; he wonders these things in relation to God's coming; God will be like a refiner's fire; God will be like a launderer's soap.

3:3: God sits; he sits as a refiner and purifier of silver; he will purify the priests; he will refine them as if they were gold and silver; at that time he will have people who will make their offerings; the offerings will be brought in a condition of righteousness.

3:4: Because of the people's righteousness (v. 3), the offerings will be acceptable; the offerings are from Judah and Jerusalem; in former years their sacrifices were acceptable.

3:5: God is speaking; he will come near to the people; he comes near to judge; he will testify against sorcerers, adulterers, perjurers, those who defraud laborers, those who oppress widows and the fatherless and those who deprive aliens of justice; these are people who do not fear the Lord; God is the Lord Almighty.

Comments: God is always described as either the one who has all power or as a judge. This is the opposite of the "God" asked about by the people in 2:17. That judge let people go free.

There are some powerful images used by or about God. Each one emphasizes either judgment or its intended result—purity.

The tone of this passage is angry, firm, direct.

Digging Deeper in Group Study

There is much colorful language in Malachi 2:17—3:5. You may have some interesting discussion centered on some of the following:

2:17: God is "wearied"

3:1: What would it be like for God to come to his temple?

3:2: "refiner's fire"

3:2: "launderer's soap"

3:3: "refiner and purifier of silver"

3:5: God will "come near"

Chapter 5: Asking Interpretive Questions

Personal Study and Reflection

Who: Under earlier prophets Haggai and Zechariah, and following the leadership of the governor Zerubbabel, the Jews had returned from exile around 500 B.C. and had rebuilt their temple. Later, under Nehemiah's leadership, they rebuilt Jerusalem as well. In Nehemiah and Ezra we see the same kinds of problems that Malachi addressed. This book was written to later-generation Jews (400 B.C.?) who were growing cold toward God. Religious formalism and even some perversion of religious expression had occurred. After the earlier excitement about returning and restoring Jerusalem to its glorious past, the people were realizing that their lot in life was to struggle under the rule of various foreign kings. They became disillusioned with their faith and either gave up on it entirely (hence such questions as "Where is the God of justice?") or settled into a cold ritualism. Interesting that their ritualism was a defense mechanism—they wanted to hold to their beliefs but they had lost faith in God. Is it any wonder that God calls himself "God Almighty" so many times? He was addressing people who had lost faith in him.

The author is simply named Malachi. Malachi means "my messenger," and it's possible that this was a title given to a nameless author. Whatever the means, God used much of the book as his own personal dialogue with his wayward people.

In this passage (2:17—3:5) there are several important protagonists: God, who speaks; Malachi, who gives commentary in 3:2-4; the nation of Judah, receivers of the message; an unwritten group, including the priests; and all evildoers listed in 3:5 who were currently getting away with evil. God and Malachi are angry, the priests and people are apathetic and sinful, the evildoers are living a godless life.

Where/When: It was noted above that the setting was Jerusalem, about 400-450 B.C. Time of writing is not specifically stated in the book.

What: There are a number of themes touched upon in this passage:

God was still willing to dialogue with his people.

The people felt that evildoers were rewarded and, inversely, that the faithful are punished.

God will send a messenger to prepare his way (John the Baptist).

He will come for two purposes: to purify and to judge.

In 3:1, it is said of the people that "you are seeking" and "you desire," yet it is apparent that their "seeking" and "desiring" of God are not from the heart.

His actions will appear in relation to the temple (that is, in the context of their faith experience).

God will set himself against all kinds of evildoers (3:5).

God will purify the priests and accept the offerings when he comes.

God is described as "weary," "Lord Almighty," "refiner's fire," "launderer's soap."

Why: Malachi wrote to faithless Jews to warn them of God's impending judgment and to promise that God would cleanse his people and his priests so that acceptable sacrifices would return to his temple.

Digging Deeper in Group Study

Questions to be answered from outside the text of Malachi 2:17—3:5:

Although various groups or individuals are mentioned in this passage, whom is God addressing, and why?

At what point in history were these words directed to the people, and what was their situation?

What is the future time spoken of in these verses? Has it happened? If not, when will it happen?

What point in history was spoken of in 3:4, when sacrifices were acceptable, and why?

If the people are truly seeking God in 3:1, then why will he come as a judge (3:2-5)?

Why is God's tone so angry?

What is meant by "judgment," "my messenger," "messenger of the covenant," "offerings in righteousness," "do not fear me"?

Chapter 6: Discovering a Passage's Structure

Personal Study and Reflection

Outline and structural analysis of Malachi 2:17—3:5

Where Is the God of Justice?

Introduction
Malachi speaks:
You   have wearied   the Lord
                with your words
The people speak:
We   have wearied   him?
                how
Malachi speaks:
You   are saying   this:
                        All who do evil are good
                                in God's eyes

and he is pleased with them
and   Where is the God
              of justice?

God speaks:
See, I   will send   my messenger
           who will prepare the way
                    before me.

the Lord   will come
  you are seeking Then
             suddenly
             to temple.
The messenger will come
     of the covenant
     whom you desire
                says the Lord Almighty.

Malachi speaks:
But who   can endure   the day
                of his coming?
Who   can stand   his appearing?
          For he will be like a refiner's fire
               a launderer's soap.
          He will sit as a refiner and purifier of silver;
          he will purify the Levites
            and refine them like gold and silver.
          Then the Lord will have men
                    who will bring offerings
                      in righteousness,
       and the offerings of Judah and Jerusalem will be acceptable
                     to the Lord
                     as in days gone by
                     as in former years.

God speaks:
See, I   will come
          near
          to you
          for judgment.
          I will testify   against sorcerers
                   quickly   adulterers
                        perjurers
                        those who defraud laborers
                        (those) who oppress widows
                              and fatherless,
                        (those who) deprive aliens
                            of justice
                        (those who) do not fear me,
                           says the Lord Almighty.

Suggestions: As you work through the outline, notice that God promises three things: "I will send my messenger," "the Lord will come to his temple and will purify" and "I will judge those who do not fear me." This will be helpful as you think about application in the next chapter.

The Jews' question in 2:17 is much more than a query about God's justice. Rooted in it is a question about their own worship. They are asking, "Where is God?" This question would affect not only their view of the world around them but their own relationship with God. As Malachi asserts, their worship has become a dead ritual precisely because they fail to see God's hand at work in their world. So God's threefold promise predicts not only judgment but God's presence as well.

Chapter 7: Making Appropriate Application

Personal Study and Reflection
Part 1: What was expected of them?
Nothing in this passage directly commands people to act one way or another. So you have to look a little beneath the surface to find application. There are three kinds of people addressed here; each perhaps has a different application.

First, Malachi addresses "the people," the average ordinary Jews. From statements in this passage and elsewhere in Malachi, they had lost confidence in God and were weakly going through the form of worship. They were slowly turning away from their God because he did not meet their expectations. They were distracted by the prosperity of those around them who got away with sinning (incidentally, the people were falling into the sin of their ancestors, who looked at the prosperity of Baal worshipers and left God for Baal). They were losing all faith in God.

Second, there were the priests, who had lost their sense of God as well. Although ministering in the temple, presumably "before the presence of the Lord," they had wandered far and become careless in their ministry.

Third, there were the evildoers. These had wandered totally from God and were to be judged. God does not seem to be even interested in addressing this group; instead he promises quick judgment against such people.

The application of this passage to the original readers seems to be one of perception first, action second. By this I mean that they are thinking wrongly of God. Their God is weak—but the real God is just. Their God is far away—but the real God is "coming near," in his temple. Their God is uninterested in their daily lives—but the real God is going to purify and cleanse. Their God is willing to let little things slip, even big things—but the real God has high expectations of them.

You will remember from chapter six that I said Malachi wrote to warn the Jews of God's judgment and impending presence.

Their response to this warning is simple: They were to repent for their lack of faith, hardheartedness and sin. And they were to turn again and follow God, loving him with heart, soul, mind and strength.

Part 2: How do I fit in?
Now, how might you and I fit into this picture? We have a profile of three different kinds of people: the lethargic Jews, the apathetic priests and the antagonistic atheists. Which are you like, and why?

How does your faith shape your life?

In what ways does your faith not produce evidence?

Are you guilty of envying hard-driving, prosperous evildoers?

Are you like the Jews in that you get caught in the form of worship and forget that you are worshiping the Lord Almighty, a Person who demands intimacy and attention?

Is your attitude toward God often harsh, accusing?

Is God far removed from your everyday life? your worship life?

Part 3: What is expected of me?
Finally, what are tools you can use to make positive steps? If I were a Jew,

I would know that time with God is a good place to start. How can you spend more time getting to know God?

Who are friends that you can tell about your decision to know God better?

How can you better prepare for worship?

What sins block your relationship with God and need to be dealt with?

How can you allow God to purify your life so that your offerings are personal and acceptable to God?

Chapter 8: Moving Beyond Application

Digging Deeper in Group Study

Questions to ponder as you meditate on Malachi 2:17—3:5:

1. What does careful analysis of "refiner's fire" reveal?

2. What happens when a person refines gold or silver?

What are parts to the process?

What are the tools employed?

What is left over from the process (dross), and what happens to it?

Imagine yourselves in God's hands as he purifies you. What is it like to feel the heat?

How does it feel to be molded and shaped by another (in other words, not your agenda, but God's)?

What must it feel like to be pure and holy, beautiful?

3. Worship is enhanced by a deep understanding of God. What does this passage teach about God?

What does it mean that God is "just"? (Note: not just judgment, but forgiveness and grace are also parts of justice.)

What does it mean that he identifies himself as the Lord Almighty?

What about the image of him purifying us *by his own hands*—and testifying personally against those who are evil?

How can each of these images draw us to God in worship?

Chapter 9: Using Inductive Methods in Group and Individual Study

Personal Study and Reflection
Abbreviated study of Malachi 3:6-12

Who: Same as 2:17—3:5 (Jews and priests of Judah), same characteristics (lack of faith, turning away from God).

What: God challenges them to return to him, especially in the area of tithing. God tells them that they are robbing him, and that he has been withholding his blessing. He promises that if they tithe he will bless them and all nations will see it.

Why: Malachi writes as God's representative, telling the people that they are to tithe to God out of faith and love, and in return they will be blessed.

Application (their response): The author says that they are to respond by bringing their whole tithe, including, we presume, healthy animals (see chapter 1) in worship.

Digging Deeper in Group Study
1. Application of Malachi 3:6-12 (our response): Is tithing still viable? Yes! Why would God say something at the end of the Old Testament time if he intended it only for a few short years before Christ? God still owns all things and makes us stewards—we in response are expected to give to his kingdom work. Our response is to freely give to God as an expression of our faith.

2. Six-week course of study through Malachi:

Week	1	Malachi 1 (focus verses 6-14)
Week	2	Malachi 2:1-9
Week	3	Malachi 2:10-16
Week	4	Malachi 2:17—3:5
Week	5	Malachi 3:6-18 (focus 6-12)
Week	6	Malachi 4

Chapter 10: Preparing and Leading an Inductive Bible Study

Personal Study and Reflection

Preparation for the learning event: Malachi 3:6-12

One-sentence purpose statement for the learning event: The purpose of this study is to explore the issue of tithing so that each disciple can respond according to his/her measure of faith.

Observation questions: Who is doing the speaking in this passage? Who is being addressed? What is God's main concern?

Interpretation questions: Why didn't the people give to God? What does it mean that they "robbed" God? What does it mean to "tithe," and why was it so important? What was God's promise if they were to tithe?

Application questions: What would God say to you about your giving? In what ways is your giving to him rooted in your love for him (see v. 7)? In what ways is it not rooted in your love for him? What is God telling you in this passage? What are you going to do about it?

Digging Deeper in Group Study

The learning event: Malachi 3:6-12

Opening questions: Recall a time when you gave kindness to somebody. How did you feel as a result? Now recall a time when you *received* kindness. How did you feel? What kind of a giver are you: grudging, hesitant, willing, joyful?

Focus questions ("heavy hitters"): Why do you think the people didn't give to God the way they should have (vv. 6-7)? Why did God use such strong language to address them in verses 8 and 9? How do you think the blessings spoken of in this passage come about?

Application: What keeps us from giving all that we should? How can we begin to give God more of what he deserves?

APPENDIX 3:
RESOURCES FOR
INDUCTIVE
STUDY

Here is a resource list to help with your inductive study.

1. Bible Versions (my preferences are starred)
King James Version (KJV): Old translation, uses formal English. Many prefer the Psalms in this version.

New King James Version (NKJV): The King James Version without the antiquated language.

*New International Version (NIV): A highly readable translation.

Revised Standard Version (RSV): Older version (since updated with the New Revised Standard); often used in mainline churches.

*New Revised Standard Version (NRSV): Updated edition of the Revised Standard Version, with changes made for gender-neutral language.

Scofield Reference Bible: Product of C. I. Scofield; a study Bible based on dispensational theology.

New American Standard Bible: Closely parallels the Hebrew and Greek; highly accurate, but the language is wooden at times.

2. Study Bibles (my preferences are starred)

*Life Application Bible: Includes introductions to books, devotional-style notes, maps and charts. A stimulating tool. Comes in several translations.

Inductive Interactive Bible: Includes space for inductive-study notes; a relatively recent publication.

*NIV Study Bible: Uses the popular NIV version, with introductions to books and commentary-style notes on each page. Answers many of the more difficult questions you would encounter in inductive study.

Scofield Reference Bible: See notes above.

Thompson Chain Reference Bible: This older study Bible lacks some of the exciting features of newer ones, but allows a student to trace themes from Genesis through Revelation through use of a creative "chain reference."

3. Bible Dictionaries

Nelson's Illustrated Bible Dictionary: One of the newer dictionaries on the market, with bright pictures and understandable definitions.

New Bible Dictionary: Informative and detailed; includes helpful maps and charts.

Vine's Expository Dictionary of New Testament Words: Valuable for word studies; uses KJV and RSV.

Zondervan Pictorial Bible Dictionary: Many contributors make this a storehouse of helpful information.

4. Bible Atlases

Macmillan Bible Atlas: An accurate atlas compiled by two Jewish scholars.

Moody Atlas of Bible Lands: Maps, pictures and diagrams of the Bible lands.

Zondervan Pictorial Bible Atlas: Includes maps with overlays to compare the political changes over the years.

5. Bible Handbooks and Helps

Eerdmans Handbook to the Bible: Has illustrations in color, is "user-friendly" and provides helpful information.

Halley's Bible Handbook: Proceeding book by book through the books of the Bible, this older resource has been useful for many years.

Nave's Topical Bible: Bible topics arranged alphabetically, with all major verses on a topic covered.

Unger's Bible Handbook: Like Halley's handbook, provides an introductory overview of the Bible and its books. Its discussion of some topics (geography, for instance) is broader than Halley's.

6. Organizations That Produce Inductive Studies for Group Use

Churches Alive! God in You Bible Study series (714) 886-5361

Harold Shaw Publishers, Fisherman Bible Study Guides (708) 665-6700

InterVarsity Press, LifeGuide® Bible Studies (800) 843-7225

NavPress, Lifechange Bible Study series (800) 525-7151

Tyndale Press, Neighborhood Bible Studies (708) 668-8300

Serendipity, Mastering the Basics, Serendipity Bible for Groups (800) 525-9563

For others, visit your local Christian bookstore.